Cambridge Elements ≡

Elements in the Archaeology of Europe
edited by
Manuel Fernández-Götz
University of Edinburgh
Bettina Arnold
University of Wisconsin–Milwaukee

A COMPARATIVE STUDY OF ROCK ART IN LATER PREHISTORIC EUROPE

Richard Bradley
University of Reading

European Association
of Archaeologists

CAMBRIDGE
UNIVERSITY PRESS

CAMBRIDGE
UNIVERSITY PRESS

University Printing House, Cambridge CB2 8BS, United Kingdom

One Liberty Plaza, 20th Floor, New York, NY 10006, USA

477 Williamstown Road, Port Melbourne, VIC 3207, Australia

314–321, 3rd Floor, Plot 3, Splendor Forum, Jasola District Centre,
New Delhi – 110025, India

79 Anson Road, #06–04/06, Singapore 079906

Cambridge University Press is part of the University of Cambridge.

It furthers the University's mission by disseminating knowledge in the pursuit of
education, learning, and research at the highest international levels of excellence.

www.cambridge.org
Information on this title: www.cambridge.org/9781108794497
DOI: 10.1017/9781108885638

First published 2020

A catalogue record for this publication is available from the British Library.

ISBN 978-1-108-79449-7 Paperback
ISSN 2632-7058 (online)
ISSN 2632-704X (print)

A Comparative Study of Rock Art in Later Prehistoric Europe

Elements in the Archaeology of Europe

DOI:10.1017/9781108885638
First published online: September 2020

Richard Bradley
University of Reading
Author for correspondence: r.j.bradley@reading.ac.uk

Abstract: This Element summarises the state of knowledge about four styles of prehistoric rock in Europe current between the late Mesolithic period and the Iron Age. They are the Levantine, Macroschematic and Schematic traditions in the Iberian Peninsula; the Atlantic style that extended between Portugal, Spain, Britain and Ireland; Alpine rock art; and the pecked and painted images found in Fennoscandia. They are interpreted in relation to the landscapes in which they were made. A final section considers possible connections between these traditions and discusses the changing subject matter of rock art in relation to wider developments in European prehistory.

Keywords: prehistory, rock art, paintings, petroglyphs, landscape

ISBNs: 9781108794497 (PB), 9781108885638 (OC)
ISSNs: 2632–7058 (online), 2632-704X (print)

Contents

1 Introduction

There are two ways of writing about European rock art. Either the text will be lengthy, detailed and cautious, or it will be shorter, optimistic and more thematic. In keeping with the format and word limit of this series, I have chosen the second course.

In most regions of Europe, the study of prehistoric rock art plays a peripheral role in archaeological research and is seldom integrated with wider discussions of the past. That is not always true – an obvious exception is work in Scandinavia – but its investigation has often been a self-contained specialism with its own meetings, institutions and publications (Bahn 2010; Bednarik 2016). Description has always been paramount and can easily become an end in itself. There has been too little awareness of chronological change and too much emphasis on subjective interpretations influenced by the literature of comparative religion (see, for instance, Anati & Fradkin 2008, and de Lumley & Echassoux 2009). Projects and their publication are often constrained by modern borders and languages. This need not be the case and I shall outline the contribution that it can make to some of the main topics of contemporary research.

For the purposes of this study, the 'later prehistoric' period extended between the Neolithic and the Iron Age. The distinctiveness of 'rock art' was explained in a recent paper by Robb (2015), who defined four of its salient features: its siting in the open air, in contrast to cave paintings which are predominantly Palaeolithic; its overlap with monumental art and statue menhirs; its close relationship with decorated objects, including pottery and metalwork; and the rarity of narrative during most phases of its existence. I shall follow his characterisation.

The literature on this subject has certain limitations. Most accounts are concerned with individual sites or regions and do not consider the wider significance of their rock art. Even fewer compare the evidence from different regions or different styles of imagery. That is because these studies are often issued as short articles. A surprisingly high proportion of the key sources appear in edited volumes, with inevitable restrictions on length and presentation.

This publication provides an up to date summary of four major styles of rock art in post-Palaeolithic Europe, supported by a large but selective bibliography. It considers the roles that these rock art styles might have played in different areas. There is also an emphasis on how their character changed over time and their relationship to other developments in later prehistory. The Iberian Peninsula is considered in Section 2, the Atlantic in Section 3, the Southern Alps and their periphery in Section 4, and Northern and Southern Scandinavia, Finland and

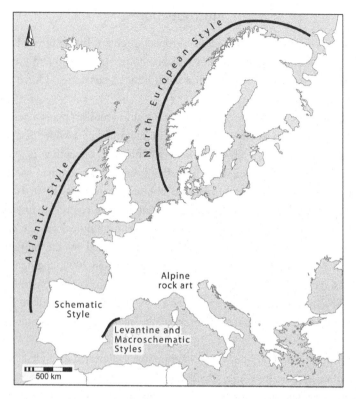

Fig. 1 Map showing the main regional styles of rock art considered in the text. Drawing: Aaron Watson

European Russia in Section 5 (Fig. 1). Smaller regional groups or single sites are excluded, including examples in Germany, Switzerland, Italy, Albania, Sardinia and Greece. The rock art of the Canary Islands is not included as it is related to that of Africa, nor are those images south of the Mediterranean which are occasionally compared with Spanish Levantine Art (Wilcox 1984). Cup marks are almost ubiquitous but play a limited role. Section 6 compares the principal traditions with one another, identifying similarities and contrasts between them over long periods of time. It argues that these distinctive images illuminate some of the most important processes in ancient society. Further information on key sites or major issues is provided in a series of text boxes; where possible, they draw on the results of projects in which I have been involved.

The study of rock art has changed in recent years. There have been important *technological developments*. Among the most informative are studies of shore-lines in Fennoscandia where the images are closely related to the sea (Ling 2013 and 2014); scientific dating of pigments or the deposits that formed over them

(Ruiz et al. 2012; López-Montalvo et al. 2014). Other initiatives have included characterisation of the paint used in making the images (Hameau 2005; Collado Giraldo et al. 2014; López Montalvo et al. 2014; Bueno Ramírez et al. 2019), the experimental replication of the motifs (Hameau & Painaud 2011; Vourc'h 2011; Lødøen 2015; Santos da Rosa 2018), and detailed survey of the areas around the decorated surfaces in order to locate structures and artefacts. An increasing number of sites are investigated by excavation.

A second development concerns *new methods of recording* the decorated panels. Painted surfaces can be enhanced using digital technology to capture images that have faded from view and to document their original colours (David et al. 2001; Brady, Hampson & Sanz 2018). Pecked motifs can also be recorded in three dimensions, together with the configuration of the surfaces on which they were created (Horn et al. 2018; Horn, Potter & Pitman 2019). This makes it easier to identify superimposed motifs. Geographic information systems help to document the views from, and between, the decorated sites and, even more importantly, their relationship to routes across the wider landscape (Fairen Jímenez 2006; Fairen Jímenez 2007; Martínez Rubío & Martorell Rubío 2012).

Lastly, rock art has been investigated using *new theoretical approaches* (Jones & Cochrane 2018; Moro Abadía & González Morale [in press]). More attention is paid to the properties of the decorated rocks and their relationship to the local topography (Bradley 2009). Were some places easier to access than others (Di Fraia 2011)? Where did people stand in order to create and observe the motifs? Some of these studies have drawn on phenomenology (Tilley 1991; Tilley 2004). At the same time there could have been a direct link between the configuration of the rock and the images made there. They can be studied in three dimensions rather than the usual two. Some panels in Northern Europe have been described as 'micro-landscapes', because their surface contours show the hills, valleys and paths followed by people and animals in the drawings (Gjerde 2010; Helskog 2014). Pictures that show the killing of whales incorporate actual pools and channels (Gjerde 2012). Similar concerns extend to the processes affecting the sites, including the relationship between the images and the movement of sunlight and water (Bradley 2009: 197–8). Advocates of the new materiality go much further, contending that any distinction between cultural and natural elements will be misleading and that the rock must be treated on equal terms with the 'art' formed on its surface (Lødøen 2010; Jones et al. 2011; Jones 2017; Goldhahn 2019a; Goldhahn 2019b: chapters 8 and 9; Fahlander 2019; Herva & Lahelma 2019). The stone should be regarded as a living being. This approach works best where there is ethnographic evidence, as there is in Fennoscandia (Lahelma 2008; Helskog 2014).

These new approaches inform the sections that follow. In this Element, I shall outline the contribution that later prehistoric rock art can make to some of the main topics of contemporary research. My account is not intended for specialists on rock art, who have concerns of their own, but for those who need to be persuaded that it can play a part in wider studies of the past. I hope that readers will find the argument convincing.

TIMES AND TRADITIONS

Robb (2015) compares the different traditions of prehistoric art in Europe between the Upper Palaeolithic period and the Iron Age. There was a distinct peak in the Neolithic phase: so much so that he suggests that it was farming that 'made us artists'. Although visual imagery had been important during earlier phases, 'expressing something that was previously fluid or ephemeral in durable materials or fixed places is not a trivial change' (2015: 640).

His study compares the chronological distribution of the images created in a variety of different media, three of which feature in this account: 'rock art', 'architectural art' and 'statuary'. Within the period considered here, rock art was usually in open settings rather than caves. Architectural art is represented by the embellishment of megalithic tombs, and most statues are anthropomorphic sculptures. An important distinction is with small figurines of fired clay or stone.

Robb's analysis explores the histories of these media. He considers the number of separate traditions documented in different parts of Europe. Two show similar trends over time, and the images characterised as 'rock art' had the same chronology as figurines, beginning between 6000 and 5000 BC, occurring in more separate styles during the fourth millennium, and becoming less common during the second; the representation of rock art recovered after 1000 BC. During the Neolithic period, architectural art showed a similar chronology to open-air rock art; a second peak was associated with complex societies in the Mediterranean and is not treated here. Lastly, between 4000 and 2000 BC, stelae were represented in a variety of regional styles. Like rock art, they also featured in the first millennium BC (Fig. 2).

The groups of rock art studied in this Element are not closely dated. This question is addressed in the separate sections, but their histories are consistent with Robb's overall scheme. The earliest were the Northern style in Fennoscandia and the Levantine Art of south-eastern Spain. In the past, both have been described as 'hunters' art' and assigned to the

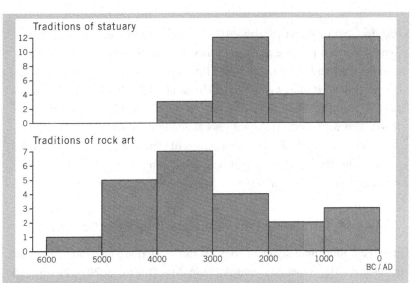

Fig. 2 The number of distinct styles of later prehistoric rock art per thousand year BC. Information from Robb (2015). Drawing: Aaron Watson

Mesolithic period. In the case of Levantine Art, the argument is controversial, but this tradition is certainly documented during the early Neolithic period. It was supplemented and eventually replaced by Iberian Schematic Art, whose chronology extended into the Copper Age and Early Bronze Age. During both phases, it was used in parallel with another style: Atlantic Art. It is less clear whether the history of Atlantic Art in Spain and Portugal extended into the first millennium BC.

The history of Alpine rock art overlapped with that of Schematic Art, with an emphasis on the Chalcolithic phase and, more locally, the Early Bronze Age. After that time, it played a smaller role, but its production was renewed on a lavish scale during the first millennium BC when it dominated the archaeological record at Valcamonica. This development has been compared with the latest manifestation of Atlantic Art and also with the sequence in South Scandinavia where the oldest images date from about 1600 BC and the most recent from the Late Bronze Age or Early Iron Age a thousand years later.

The distributions of some traditions overlapped, but others remained largely separate. Rock art and figurines may share similar chronologies, but for the most part they are found in completely different regions. The figurines were mainly a feature of Central and Eastern Europe where rock art was poorly represented, but they do occur in the Copper Age and Early

Bronze Age of Iberia (Scarre 2017). By contrast, the images associated with decorated passage graves overlap with the Schematic Art of Spain and Portugal and the Atlantic Art of Britain, Ireland and the north-west of Iberia (Bueno Ramirez & Balbín Behrmann 2000; Bradley 2009; Alves 2012). In north-western France and the Iberian Peninsula, the images associated with megalithic tombs are found in the same regions as statue menhirs. In the same way, the distribution of Copper Age and Bronze Age rock art in the Alps overlapped with the anthropomorphic stelae of the same periods, but only at Valcamonica were their elements combined.

2 Rock Art in the Iberian Peninsula: Images in Contention

There were four main styles of rock art in the Iberian Peninsula: Levantine, Macroschematic, Schematic and Atlantic Arts (Lillios 2020, 149–56). The first three are considered in this section, but the fourth, which was once termed 'Galician', formed part of a more extensive tradition discussed in Section 3 (Fig. 3).

The first of these, *Levantine Art*, is defined both geographically and stylistically (García Arranz, Collado Giraldo & Nash 2012; Lillios 2020, 150–6).

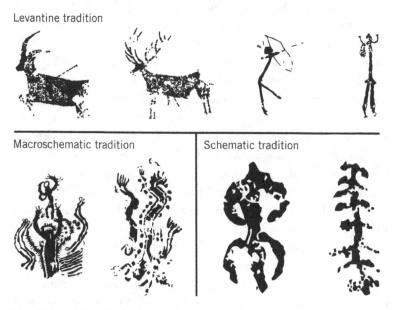

Fig. 3 Typical motifs in Levantine, Macroschematic and Schematic Art. Information from Fairén Jiménez (2006). Drawing: Aaron Watson

Its distribution is restricted to south-east Spain. All the images were painted and were characterised by hunters, wild animals, dancers and scenes of foraging and fighting. Unlike the other styles, it is essentially figurative. Some scenes include one dominant creature (Bea & Rojo 2013), and there was an obvious emphasis on masculinity (Escoriza Mateu 2008). The contents of these panels became increasingly violent over time (López-Montalvo 2015).

Research in the Iberian Peninsula was influenced by studies of earlier cave paintings, and Breuil (1933–5) investigated both genres. Because of its emphasis on hunting and wild animals, Levantine Art was connected with Palaeolithic images. There could have been stylistic links between them. The paintings described as Levantine Art have been compared with the drawings of early postglacial origin (Bueno Ramírez & Balbín Behrmann 2016). It remains uncertain whether there was any hiatus between the last images created during the Palaeolithic period and those dated to the Neolithic.

The styles of *Macroschematic* and *Schematic Art* are much less clearly defined. To some extent they overlap, and their very names are unhelpful. Schematic Art had a lengthy history and included a wide variety of painted and pecked motifs (Breuil 1933–5; Acosta 1968; Fairén Jiménez 2015). Macroschematic Art, on the other hand, may have been less diverse (Hernández Pérez 2006). Its distribution was similar to that of Levantine Art, while Schematic Art is recorded almost everywhere in Iberia apart from the far north-west. Today, rock paintings are more common to the south and pecked imagery to the north (Fig. 4). There was a similar distinction in megalithic art which corresponds to two climatic zones, one more favourable to the preservation of pigment (Devignes 1997). Both Macroschematic and Schematic Arts combined figurative and abstract images and were distinguished from one another by size and sometimes by chronology. New images may have been added to older ones, and others were altered over time (Fairén Jiménez 2006; Cruz Berrocal & Vicent García 2007). With a few exceptions, they did not constitute compositions or 'scenes'.

There were certain contrasts. As its name suggests, Macroschematic Art included significantly larger images than Schematic Art. The most diagnostic were strange composite creatures which included humans merging with animals or other beings. Schematic Art, on the other hand, favoured abstract signs, dots and bars, wild animals, weapons, axes, miniature humans, eyes (*oculi*), handprints and depictions of the sun. There was considerable variation between individual sites and panels. The distribution of these elements was studied by Acosta (1968) who drew on the publications of Breuil. She showed that there were local variations, and the images themselves could have been made at different times.

Fig. 4 Painted figures in the Schematic style at Peña Piñeda, Vega de
Espinareda, Spain. Photograph: Lara Bacelar Alves

Chronology

Levantine Art, with its depictions of people and wild animals, may have
originated in the Epipalaeolithic: a view supported by a small number of
radiocarbon and optically stimulated luminescence dates (Bueno Ramírez,
Balbín Behrmann & Barroso Bermejo 2012; Bueno Ramírez & Balbín
Behrmann 2016; Lillios 2020, 153–4). There are other sources of information
for Levantine Art: the types of arrowhead depicted in the paintings (Fernández
López de Pablo 2006); the use of milk products in the pigment (Roldán et al.
2018); and a few scenes supposedly portraying tame animals (Bea & Pajas
2016). All three features suggest that it was being made during the Neolithic
phase. The same applies to Macroschematic Art which shared the same designs
as Impressed Ware dating from the earliest Neolithic period (Fernández López
de Pablo 2014; Binder et al. 2017). Similarly, Schematic Art resembled the
decoration inside a few Iberian passage tombs (Bueno Ramírez & Balbín
Behrmann 2000; Bueno Ramírez, Balbín Behrmann & Barroso Bermejo
2009; Bueno Ramírez, Balbín Behrmann & Barroso Bermejo 2015), the distinctive pottery known as *Symbolkeramik* (Martín Socas & Camalich Massieu
1982), occasional Bell Beaker ceramics, and a series of engraved plaques and
'idols' (Lillios 2004; Hurtado Perez 2008). Lillios (2008) dates the plaques
between 3500 BC and the Beaker phase in the mid to late third millennium BC.
There are radiocarbon dates for painted *oculi* in the mid fourth millennium

(Ruiz et al. 2012), and those for the idols also fall in the later fourth and the earlier third millennia BC. This evidence suggests that Schematic Art was current between the Early Neolithic and the Early Bronze Age and that it outlasted the other traditions.

The situation is more complicated because of the relationship between these styles in south-east Spain (Fairén Jiménez 2006). Here, diagnostic images from all three groups might be superimposed or their positions juxtaposed with respect to one another on the same sites (Hernández Pérez 2006: fig. 13); Fernández López de Pablo 2014). The problem is that this did not happen in a consistent order. Thus Levantine Art could overlie Macroschematic or Schematic Art, or they could be located on separate parts of the same panel. Because of the link between Macroschematic Art and decorated pottery, it has been implied that Levantine Art was a wholly Neolithic phenomenon but in that case it is difficult to explain the emphasis on hunting and the wild. If it had an earlier beginning, might these superimpositions have occurred at a later stage in the history of this style?

Distribution

Schematic Art extended across most parts of the Iberian Peninsula, into the south of France (Hameau 2002), and, on a more local scale, to Italy (Matteoli 2012; Cremonisi & Tosatti 2017). The distributions of Levantine and Macroschematic Arts overlapped with Schematic Art in south-east Spain but reached no further, supporting the argument that the latter style lasted a longer time (Martínez García & Hernández Pérez 2000). It complemented the Atlantic Art of the north-west whose date is still disputed (Alves & Comendador Rey 2018). There could be local contrasts in the selection of sites in all three traditions, but it remains to account for the frequency of superimpositions. Why was it so important in landscapes where equally suitable locations could be found nearby?

Locations

Studies employing geographic information systems suggest that sites with rock art could be situated between settlements but were rarely linked directly to them (Cruz Berrocal 2005). On the other hand, they were usually close to paths (Martínez i Rubio & Martorell Briz 2012). There were local preferences for rock shelters or caves. Despite evidence for the intermittent use of these places, artefacts are rarely found, and there were comparatively few direct links between Schematic Art and human burials. Closer connections are indicated where motifs in the same style were associated with megalithic tombs (Bueno

Ramírez & Balbín Behrmann 2000; Bueno Ramírez, Balbín Behrmann & Barroso Bermejo 2013).

All three styles favoured cliffs, rock shelters and outcrops (Sanches & Morais 2011; Collado Giraldo 2016). Some of them were difficult to access or had restricted space – the name of one site translates as 'the Frieze of Terror' (Collado Giraldo et al. 2014) – but others were much easier to reach (Fairén Jiménez 2006). River margins were important too, especially those of the Tagus and Guadiana (Bueno Ramírez, Balbín Behrmann & Barroso Bermejo 2008; Alves 2012). They are not fully documented as many examples are submerged today (Gomes 1983), but new research links many of the images with Schematic Art (Collado Giraldo 2006; Garcês and Oosterbeek 2020). Rock art of every kind could be associated with routes across the upland landscape (Collado Giraldo 2016) and, in certain cases, the sites commanded extensive views. For example, a decorated rock shelter at the important site of Menga was close to an enormous passage grave and faced an anthropomorphic mountain (Rogerio-Candelera et al. 2018). Some of the panels would have been as difficult to paint as they are for archaeologists to record. Indeed Hameau (2007) suggests that the topography provided a kind of 'natural architecture' and that certain locations were chosen specifically because they were secluded.

Interpretations

To differing extents, Levantine Art and Schematic Art featured hunting scenes, and it is true that the bones of wild animals are found in inland areas throughout the Neolithic period (López-Montalvo 2018). The association between decorated sites and summer grazing in the historical era suggests that domesticates should have been illustrated too, but, like Levantine Art, Schematic Art seems to have depicted a masculine world typified by wild animals and occasional drawings of weapons (Escoriza Mateu 2008). It also included more specialised elements – *oculi*, geometric patterns recalling the decoration of schist plaques, and depictions of the sun. The positions of sites with rock art could be influenced by natural features and processes. They included the presence of thermal springs or percolating water (Hameau 2003; Oosterbeck 2009). There was a local preference for the use of red rock or red concretions (Hameau 2005); again, the pigment was often red (Rogiero Candelera et al. 2018). Other common elements were outcrops containing quartz veins, locations where sound was amplified, and places with echoes (Mattioli et al. 2017). Caves and shelters with paintings of the sun might be illuminated at the solstices: a typical example is the aptly named Cueva del Sol near Cádiz. Almost 60 per cent of the sites depicting the sun faced south, compared with 30 per cent of the decorated sites in which this image did not occur (Versaci 2019). These places may have been visited on special occasions and some could have been used in rites of passage (Hameau & Painaud 2009).

The presence of certain panels may be associated with hunting and keeping livestock, and their distribution could have reflected patterns of land use. This did not apply to all of them and Levantine Art occurred at a few locations dominated by outsize images (Bea & Rojo 2013). They may have included large aggregation sites (Fairén Jiménez 2015). Schematic Art could assume an equally specialised role. *Symbolkeramik* and occasional Bell Beakers were decorated with similar designs to rock art and were associated with large walled settlements (Bradley 2009, 215). A similar argument may apply to the embellishment of megalithic tombs where the deepest space might include specialised images resembling the decoration of statue menhirs (Bueno Ramírez & Balbín Behrmann 2000). There was probably a continuum in the repertoire of Schematic Art which extended between the supposedly sacred and mundane worlds, yet in some cases the most complex imagery occurred where space was restricted and access was particularly difficult (Hameau 2007).

The Wider Context

Rock art illuminates at least two themes in the archaeology of Iberia and the West Mediterranean.

Firstly, new research has documented the rapid colonisation of the coast by immigrant farmers, an interpretation supported by ancient DNA from human bones (García de Lagrán, Fernández Domínguez & Rojo Guerra 2018; Shennan 2018, chapter 5; Olalde et al. 2019; Lillios 2020, 109–29). Pockets of fertile soil were settled, leaving less promising spaces in between them (Manem 2014). *If* Levantine Art was first made by local hunter-gatherers, how can we explain its interaction with the other styles? Perhaps one clue is provided by the increasing number of panels showing violent conflict (López-Montalvo 2015). It may be important that this style is rare or absent in areas settled by the earliest immigrants, whose activities expanded into the hinterland over time. That is where most of the rock art is found. It has always been a problem to explain why images in up to three different styles were superimposed or juxtaposed, and why the same sites were used (López de Pablo 2014; Martí Oliver & Bernabeu Aubán 2014). Does it reflect the interaction between two populations: one indigenous and the other non-local? In that case, the right comparison may be with contact period art in other parts of the world in which visual imagery is one way of asserting claims to places, histories and ways of life (Goldhahn &

May 2019). Might that account for what appear to be confrontations between the different styles?

Secondly, it has long been accepted that Schematic Art was allied with monumental architecture, but until recently the focus was on motifs shared with artefacts from tombs and two groups of walled settlements: Los Millares and its neighbours in the south of Iberia, and those in the west of Portugal (Jorge 2003; Lillios 2020, 174–86 and 201–10). Other references may have been to schist plaques, idols, *Symbolkeramik* and Bell Beaker pottery. New work shows that the walled sites were more widely distributed than originally supposed and that there were extensive ditched enclosures too (Jiménez Jáimez 2015; Lillios 2020, 186–9). Indeed, complexes like Zambujal were far larger than first thought (Kunst 2017). In a few cases, there appears to be a link between such sites and 'sanctuaries' with Schematic Art. In other cases, this suggests that control of territory reached further than previously thought and that rituals performed in liminal areas may have been part of the same developments as activities at these monuments. They are epitomised by the spread of Bell Beakers and by the occasional overlap between ceramic decoration and the same motifs in rock art.

PASSOS / SANTA COMBA MOUNTAIN, PORTUGAL

Passos Mountain is a conspicuous landmark, rising above a lowland basin to a height of 1000 m (Fig. 5). It can be seen from all directions, but, viewed from below, its most striking feature is a large cave (Buraco da Pala) just below the summit (Fig. 6). On excavation, it provided important chronological and structural evidence. Survey in the surrounding area has identified a series of rock shelters in the valleys that provide access to the high ground. Like the cave on the mountaintop, over a dozen of these shelters preserve painted panels of Schematic Art. They occur in two main

Fig. 5 Passos / Santa Comba Mountain, Portugal. Photograph: Lara Bacelar Alves

Fig. 6 The cave of Buraco da Pala, Portugal . Photograph: Lara Bacelar Alves

clusters, each associated with a different route up the mountain. There are four outliers. There may have been an open settlement nearby but no structural evidence survives (Sanches & Morais 2011).

Buraco de Pala has an unusual character. Not only is it a striking topographical feature, there was a natural amphitheatre in front of its entrance that could have accommodated a large number of people. Although it can be interpreted as a living site, it had several unusual characteristics. The sequence extended from the Neolithic period, through the Copper Age into the Early Bronze Age, and the cave contained a large number of artefacts. They included non-local materials such as variscite and gold, there was evidence of metal production, and among the exca-vated ceramics were vessels with similar decoration to Symbolkeramik. The structural evidence was even more striking, for much of the internal space was used to store cereals and other foodstuffs. Some were kept on wooden racks, but the majority were held in ceramic containers. The excavator distinguished between this zone with its evidence for food storage and a significantly smaller domestic area characterised by numerous hearths, some of them used only briefly. In contrast to the area where consumables were stored, this part of the site was associated with small vessels suitable for serving food and drink. The simplest interpretation is that Buraco da Pala was an aggregation site visited on special occasions and that feasts had taken place there. By a curious coincidence, that it is how the site was used in recent centuries when it became a sanctuary visited by Christian pilgrims (Sanches et al. 1998).

Buraco da Pala itself contained few painted motifs. In this respect, it contrasted with the more lavishly decorated shelters on the flanks of the mountain where the images in shallow caves even extended to the roof. Taken together, they account for much of the repertoire of Iberian Schematic Art, and a few motifs resemble designs found as far away as south-east Spain. They include ovals and rectangles filled with parallel lines, bars, dots, branching forms resembling trees, stars, eyes (oculi), and drawings of human figures (Fig 7). Animals and weapons were not represented.

The main group of sites with Schematic Art is on either side of a valley which leads up the mountain from the south east, and these places command views over the surrounding lowlands rather than the higher ground. Compared with Buraco da Pala, these sites are comparatively small and could never accommodate many people. They are associated with distinctive landforms, including cliffs, and several are difficult to reach. They may have been selected for that reason. There are striking contrasts between them. The most elaborate panels employed pigments of different colours from the rest, and neighbouring sites could share the same kinds of images. The most complex featured oculi and were only 50 m apart.

These were not the only rock shelters on Passos Mountain but the rest contained fewer painted motifs and some were never decorated. That is particularly striking as these particular sites can be associated with prehistoric artefacts. In fact, those on the mountainside were used in at least two ways. The painted shelters were special and comparatively inaccessible and they do not seem to have been occupied. By contrast, the sites without these images may have played a less restricted role and they were the ones that provide evidence of occupation. It seems clear that in this case Schematic Art did play a specialised role.

Fig. 7 Schematic motifs in cave and rock shelters around Passos /
Santa Comba Mountain, Portugal. Information from Sanches
and Morais (2011). Drawing: Aaron Watson

EL PEDROSO, SPAIN

El Pedroso is a granite mountain overlooking the Spanish Meseta to the
east and the high ground of northern Portugal to the west (Alves, Bradley
& Fábregas Valcarce 2013; Lillios 2020, 215–16). It was occupied during
the Chalcolithic and Early Bronze Age when a defended enclosure was
built on its summit, associated with a monumental entrance, several
bastions or towers, and a series of circular houses. On its lower slopes
are terraces with evidence of prehistoric activity. One was revetted by
a wall and located at the foot of a conspicuous granite outcrop (Fig. 8).
Beneath the rock there was a cave with two chambers connected to one
another by a narrow passage. Both were embellished with petroglyphs.
The motifs nearest to the entrance consisted almost exclusively of cup
marks; they also extended into the first section of the passage, which at
some stage had been partly blocked. The second chamber, which was lit by

Fig. 8 The granite outcrop and decorated cave at El Pedroso,
Spain. Photograph: Richard Bradley

sunlight percolating through natural openings in the roof, contained
a series of panels featuring anthropomorphs and handprints (Fig. 9).
How were the separate groups of petroglyphs related to one another?

Excavation on the external terrace established a stratigraphic sequence
associated with diagnostic artefacts. It also provided evidence of at least
one oven and the construction of a stone platform with a wooden super-
structure which had been destroyed by fire between 2650 and 2450 BC.
There was no indication of any houses. These deposits extended into the
mouth of the cave. Despite considerable disturbance, they provided evidence for continuous or discontinuous use between approximately
3000 BC and the first half of the second millennium BC.

Quite different material was excavated in the rear chamber of the cave
which was decorated almost exclusively with Schematic Art. Here there
were two phases of activity. The first was in the late third millennium BC
when a Palmela point (a type of copper arrowhead) was deposited there,
presumably accompanying a burial destroyed by the acid subsoil. There
was also a variscite bead. The second was during the Early Bronze Age

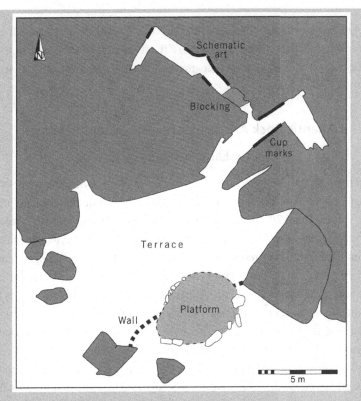

Fig. 9 Outline plan of the decorated cave at El Pedroso, Spain. Information from Alves, Bradley and Fàbregas Valcarce 2013

when large numbers of ceramic vessels suitable for serving food and drink accumulated in this small space. This recalls the evidence from Buraco de Pala.

Certain contrasts seem to be important. The assemblage associated with the first chamber and the finds from the platform included large storage vessels and might provide evidence of domestic activities. That is not surprising as cup marks like those in the entrance are found at settlements in other parts of Spain. The images in the deepest part of the cave had a more specialised character, although many of them had been altered during the Christian era. The rear chamber at El Pedroso may originally have been occupied by a burial, but in a later phase it could have been employed in other ways. Now it was a secluded location where transactions could be conducted in secrecy. Special attention was paid to the cave at a time when local passage graves were reused, and this site was treated in similar ways to those monuments. Like those megalithic structures, it possessed a forecourt, a passage and a principal chamber, and, in common with some of those structures, the mouth of the cave was embellished with cup marks. There were more specialised motifs in the interior.

3 Atlantic Rock Art: Contacts with Distant Relations

Early Research

The term Atlantic rock art refers to a series of local styles shared between Portugal, Spain, Ireland and Britain (Bradley 1997; Balbín Behrmann et al; 2009; Valdez-Tullet 2019), although there have been claims – not yet systematically evaluated – of links with further images in the Alps and even Scandinavia (Santos Estévez 2013; Fredell 2010). Initial work defined one non-figurative style in the north, and another (supplemented by drawings of weapons, humans, animals and artefacts) in the south. A specifically British and Irish style was first identified in the nineteenth century (Simpson 1867). The southern element was originally described as the 'Galician' style, but its significance was obscured because the first corpus was published in Latin (Sobrino Buhigas 1935). It is better to refer to it as 'Atlantic Art'. Links between these two regions were first discussed in MacWhite (1946). Now it is recognised that this style extends from Spain down the Portuguese coast (Alves 2012; Alves & Commendador Rey 2018).

Vocabulary

The abstract element was essentially an elaboration of cup marks which were widely distributed, sometimes in isolation (Fig. 10). There was animal art to the south which perhaps overlapped with Schematic Art, and both the styles could be combined on individual sites. Recent work has identified a few paintings (Rodríguez Rallán, Fábregas Valcarce & Carrera Ramírez in press). Weapons occurred much more widely among the petroglyphs, including those in Iberia (Fábregas Valcarce, Rodríguez Rellán & Rodríguez Alvarez 2011), Scotland and southern England (Bradley 1998). They were also represented on stelae of various dates. Curvilinear motifs are common towards the west coast of Iberia where they can be found in isolation (Fig. 11). Drawings of animals, often combined with these images, are more frequent in the hinterland, but it is not clear whether they were a secondary development.

An important concept is 'arming the landscape' (Fábregas Valcarce et al. 2007; Rodríguez-Corral 2019). There were drawings of weapons in the

Fig. 10 Cup marks and related motifs at Cacharelas, Spain. Photograph: Ramon Fàbregas Valcarce

Fig. 11 Circular motifs overlooking the Atlantic coast of Spain. Photograph: Ramon Fàbregas Valcarce

north-west of Spain from the late third millennium BC – these places have been characterised as 'armed rocks' and can feature both daggers and halberds. In a subsequent phase, statue menhirs were equipped with weapons, and in this case the artefacts were associated with a human body. The Late Bronze Age stelae of south-west Iberia were more explicitly anthropomorphic (Díaz-Guardamino 2010 and 2014). Such images show evidence of alteration.

By contrast, it is accepted that Atlantic art in Scotland and Ireland overlapped with tomb decoration (as was the case with Iberian Schematic Art). Close connections between open-air rock art in Portugal, Spain, Ireland and Britain are demonstrated by its design grammar and the ways of forming the images (Valdez-Tullet 2019). The main features were cups, circles, radial lines and basins. Some were simple designs, but others were visually elaborate, with different motifs joined together to form complex panels (Fig. 12). In Galicia, there are regional variations in their distribution and contents (Rodríguez Rellán, Vazquez Martínez & Fábregas Valcarce 2018). British and Irish non-figurative designs also show local patterning, but here it was less pronounced (Sharpe 2012), and in this case the main contrast was between areas dominated by cup marks and those with cups and rings (Jones & Kirkham 2013). In Britain, there were only a few depictions of Early Bronze Age metalwork, mainly axeheads but also daggers and a single halberd. All were directly associated with monuments, the best known of which is Stonehenge (Bradley 1998).

Fig. 12 Circular motifs and other non-figurative designs at Beira da Costa, Spain. Photograph: Ramon Fàbregas Valcarce

Distribution

In Iberia this style was best represented around the *rías* (the estuaries discharging into the Atlantic), along the main rivers and paths leading into the interior, and in moist basins (*brañas*) in the hinterland (Rodríguez Rellán, Gorgoso López & Fábregas Valcarce 2008; Fábregas Valcarce & Rodríguez Rellán 2012a; Santos Estévez 2013). This changed around the Spanish/Portuguese border, and the style once considered to be specifically Galician extends southwards for another 150 km (Alves 2012; Bettencourt et al. 2017). In fact, one of the largest concentrations of non-figurative imagery overlooks the modern frontier at the River Miño from the high ground to its south (Alves & Reis 2017). New work shows that it extends further inland than was originally supposed (Rodríguez Rellán, Gorgoso López & Fábregas Valcarce 2008). Atlantic rock art was almost absent on the north coast of Spain and in western France, but cup marks did occur widely. Like their counterparts in northwestern Europe, the panels incorporated the surface features of the rock. The drawings of weapons in Iberia adopted more conspicuous positions than the others, and some were on steeply sloping surfaces which seem to confront the viewer (Fábregas Valcarce, Rodríguez Rellán & Rodríguez Alvarez 2011). Like the more complex non-figurative motifs, they could also be near the sea (Santos Estévez & Güimil Fariña 2015; Rodríguez Rellán, Vazquez Martínez & Fábregas Valcarce 2018). There were rare drawings of armed figures like those illustrated on freestanding stelae (Rodríguez-Corral 2019).

The situation was very different in Britain and Ireland. Non-figurative rock art occurred mainly in northern England, central, eastern and western Scotland and in two main concentrations in the north and south-west of Ireland (Bradley 1997: fig. 5.1; O'Connor 2006). Elsewhere, cup marks predominated, for instance in northern Scotland, Wales and south-west England (Jones & Kirkham 2013). The same applied to Finistère, where they were sometimes reused in stone-built monuments (Pailler & Nicolas 2016). Decorated panels appeared in major concentrations close to henges or settings of monoliths (Bradley 1997, chapter 7; Jones et al. 2011). Standing stones were also decorated in the same style, although it is not clear whether some of them had been recycled. Chance finds suggest that Atlantic Art extended to more perishable surfaces in lowland England, and a few related motifs can be found on portable artefacts (Jones & Díaz Guardamino 2019).

Chronology

There are several options. The chronology of the northern component depends on comparisons with Irish megalithic art, occasional motifs in Late Neolithic stone buildings like those at the Ness of Brodgar in Orkney, and artefact decoration (Thomas 2016; Bueno Ramírez et al. 2019; Jones & Díaz Guardamino 2019). At Loughcrew, fragments of already-decorated rock taken from a nearby outcrop seem to have been incorporated in a passage tomb (Shee Twohig et al. 2010). Related motifs are found occasionally on stone circles or standing stones dating from the late third and early second millennia BC. In Britain and Ireland, detached pieces of already-decorated rock were reused in the structure of Chalcolithic and Early Bronze Age stone-lined graves (*cists*) (Bradley 1997: chapter 9). This provides a *terminus ante quem*, but they were reused in a way that shows a familiarity with the original design grammar and a preference for motifs shared with passage grave art. There were few special-ised motifs in the open air, but Frodsham (1996) has identified a striking association between pecked spirals, the choice of red stone for embellishment, and the use of vertical surfaces. Occasionally there are associations between open-air art, finds of Arran pitchstone (a kind of Scottish obsidian), and Late Neolithic Grooved Ware; related motifs have been recognised on stone plaques and other objects. Those featuring spirals and nested arcs are also found in Irish passage graves dating from the end of the fourth millennium BC (Jones & Díaz Guardamino 2019).

There are indications of a longer history. Early Bronze Age monuments, a few with radiocarbon dates, include large cup marks, some with very slight rings (Bradley & Watson 2019). They are occasionally associated with draw-ings of early axeheads and daggers. In Britain, the last cup-marked stones found in reliable contexts date from the Middle Bronze Age (Bradley 1997: 146–8). In south-west Ireland, they also feature on Early and Middle Bronze Age monu-ments (O' Brien 2012: chapter 5). Although more complex panels with curvi-linear motifs occurred in the same region, they do not appear to have been reused.

The southern component may have had a different history, with an early phase overlapping with Irish megalithic art (Fábregas Valcarce 2009). In this case the main argument is stylistic. Its distribution complements that of Iberian Schematic Art to the south and east. A second phase is dated by drawings of idols and Chalcolithic/Early Bronze Age metalwork which are sometimes represented on the same surface; a recent paper dates Iberian halberds between 2500 and 2000 BC (Needham 2015). After that time, weapons were depicted on freestanding stelae and date from the later second and first millennia BC.

It has been suggested that petroglyphs showing hunters on horseback may be Late Bronze Age or Iron Age. They are less frequent than scenes of people hunting on foot, but the case depends on comparison with the better-dated Alpine rock art (Santos Estévez & Seoane Veiga 2010; Santos Estévez 2013).

The excavated evidence is not decisive, and arguments are also based on the ages of identifiable artefacts or images found in other regions. They include: 'palettes' (perhaps a kind of mirror), wheel crosses, swastikas, labyrinths, and the 'Cammunan rose': a distinctive motif associated with the Iron Age phase in Valcamonica (Quintas González & Espejo Guardiola 2008). More depends on the first evidence of horse riding in Iberia (Fàbregas Valcarce, Peña Santos & Rodríguez Rellán 2011; Bendrey 2012; Fages et al. 2019). These issues are still being debated, but there are Atlantic-style drawings of horses on the wall of the Iron Age *oppidum* of Yecla de Yeltes in Salamanca (Martín Valls 1983). In north-west Spain and Portugal there is even some continuity of site with Late Bronze Age/Iron Age hillforts (Rey Castiñeira & Soto Barreiro 2001; Dinis & Bettencourt 2011).

Thus different researchers favour *either* a short chronology *or* a long one for Atlantic rock art in Iberia. The short chronology focuses on the early metal age and the few finds from sites in north-west Iberia including early metalwork and Chalcolithic/Early Bronze Age pottery (Seoane Veiga, Prieto Martínez & Dal Zovo 2013; Fábregas Valcarce & Rodríguez Rellán 2015: table 5.2). The long chronology is plausible but will be difficult to prove. Finally, these panels were altered when the sites were Christianised. Writing in 1968, Anati confused medieval and later motifs with the repertoire of Iberian Schematic Art (Costas Goberna & Novoa Álvarez 1993: 231–3; Rodríguez Rellán, Gorgoso López & Fábregas Valcarce 2008).

To sum up a confusing situation, in the north parallels with Irish passage grave art provide a minimum age of 3300 – 2900 BC for components of Atlantic rock art. Reuse of already-decorated fragments in the Early Bronze Age shows some appreciation of their original significance. Drawings of weapons can be found with cup marks and the sequence closes about 1500 BC. In the south, the origins of this style should also be in the fourth millennium BC (Alves 2012). Its distribution avoids that of Schematic Art and the two styles must have overlapped with one another in time, although their histories need not have coincided completely. In Spain and Portugal, petroglyphs may have been created over a longer period, and here their chronology depends on analogy with Alpine sites where many of the motifs were superimposed. The distribution of Galician sites complements that of statue menhirs in northern Portugal which were made from the second millennium BC onwards.

Locations

In south-west Europe there was an emphasis on inland routeways, river valleys and upland basins which may have been occupied seasonally. Some settlements were nearby, but others were more distant. Excavation has not encountered many artefacts around the decorated surfaces (Santos Estévez & Criado Boado 2000; Criado Boado, Martínez Cortizas & García Quintela 2013; Seoane Veiga, Prieto Martínez & Dal Zovo 2013). For the most part, rock art avoided prominent outcrops or peaks, but this changed towards the south with a greater emphasis on three-dimensional panels rather than horizontal surfaces. Here hilltops may have been more important (Bettencourt et al. 2017). Throughout its distribution, there have been new discoveries of decorated rock shelters (Fábregas Valcarce & Rodríguez Rellán 2012 a). The sites with rock art were not always visible from paths, as was once believed (Fábregas Valcarce & Rodríguez Rellán 2012b; Rodríguez Rellán & Fábregas Valcarce 2016). Some of the curvilinear motifs were integrated with drawings of animals, suggesting that they represented elements of the local topography (Fig. 13).

The situation was different in Britain and Ireland where there was an emphasis on paths, basins and passes. Rock art was often associated with viewpoints and the edges of settled land (Bradley 1997, 79–89). A study using GIS showed that the rock art of Northumberland in north-east England was located in places raised between 25 and 45 m above the surrounding area. They were on shallowly sloping ground. These positions could be recognised from 2 km away even if the outcrop itself was invisible. These

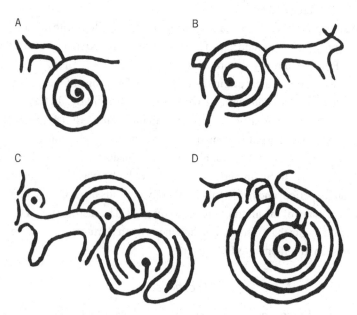

Fig. 13 Drawings of animals entering or leaving circular designs in Iberian Atlantic art. Information from Bradley (1997). Drawing: Aaron Watson

sites also overlooked routes across the surrounding country (Fairén Jiménez 2007). In south-west Ireland, the more complex designs referenced important estuaries providing access to the hinterland (Westlake 2005), and, in Britain, the most ornate panels could be found on higher ground than the main concentrations of cup marks (Bradley 1997: 79–88). In north-east England, cup-marked rocks followed the limits of cairnfields interpreted as patches of agricultural land (Deakin 2007)). They also occur at a few Early Bronze Age barrow cemeteries (Vyner 2007). Complex designs incorporated rarer motifs shared with megalithic tombs and were obviously influenced by the configuration of the rock, in particular its colours, textures, glacial cracks and fissures (Jones et al. 2011: Enlander 2016). Little use was made of prominent outcrops, peaks, rock shelters or caves. In Britain and Ireland, at least some of the major finds were around ceremonial centres and the routes leading towards them (Bradley 1997: 113–20; O'Connor 2006; Jones et al. 2011). There is little evidence that individual panels were altered. While the images must have built up over time, successive motifs usually respected one another.

Solar references may have been significant in the main regions with Atlantic Art. Many sites commanded views of the sky and featured prominent circular motifs. Decorated passage graves in Ireland may have influenced this pattern as about a fifth of them were aligned on the rising or setting sun at the solstices (Prendergast et al. 2017). In Britain, the pecked designs on decorated outcrops might contain mineral inclusions that sparkled in strong light. Quartz was extracted at one of the decorated outcrops in Scotland (Bradley & Watson 2019). Worked stone was deposited in natural cracks at rock art sites (Jones et al. 2011; Bradley, Watson, & Anderson-Whymark 2013; Bradley & Watson 2019), and there are finds of metalwork from their counterparts in western Iberia (Alves & Comendador Rey 2009).

Interpretations

How important was Atlantic rock art? It depends on its social setting. In the north, it was closely related to monuments and the dead. It was also a focus for smaller, more informal deposits. It may have played a part in the demarcation of territory as areas of the landscape were occupied for the first time since the Mesolithic period. The same may have happened in south-west Europe where there might even have been some cross references between the distinctive profiles of the decorated rocks and those of mountains in the wider landscape. Drawings of animal tracks suggest a similar idea, but their date is uncertain.

In one sense, the main Irish passage graves provided microcosms of a larger region. They were built out of raw materials assembled from an enormous area and their characteristic decoration combined the angular motifs associated with artefacts and dwellings with the curvilinear elements that featured in the wider landscape (Bradley 2009: 112–22). The combination of cups and rings might have referred to the architecture of these tombs. Here the radial line is the crucial element for it can be construed as a path entering the stone. This motif is confined to *open-air* rock art and is not represented at monuments where a real passage leads into a chamber. That is particularly revealing as curvilinear designs – both circles and spirals – are frequently recorded around the entrances of Irish megaliths (Dronfield 1996; Robin 2009). This would suggest that the commonest 'abstract' motif recorded in open-air rock art referred to the same *idea* as the layout of a passage grave, but this is a rather literal interpretation. 'Tunnel imagery' features in accounts of the subjective visions experienced in altered states of consciousness (Lewis-Williams & Dowson 1988), but such claims are controversial and it is difficult to take the argument further in the space available here.

The Significance of Atlantic Rock Art

The problem is to explain the similarities between distant areas. There seem to be three possible contexts for the first connections between these regions.

One was the movement of jadeitite axes from the western Alps (Pétrequin et al. 2012; Pétrequin, Pétrequin & Gauthier 2017). Although their distribution connected Iberia, Brittany, Britain and Ireland, the links seem to have extended from the Alps first to north-west France and then southwards to Iberia. These connections were at an end by the early fourth millennium BC, and the imported artefacts in England and Scotland could be among the last examples. They seem too early to be relevant to this account.

Atlantic passage graves may have been a more significant influence, but the decorated tombs in Ireland which recall motifs in the wider landscape were later than their supposed equivalents in Brittany, and direct comparisons based on megalithic art along the coastline are confined to a few sites and designs (O' Sullivan 1997; Bueno Ramírez et al. 2019). Eogan (1990) has postulated Iberian origins or inspiration for artefacts associated with monuments in the Boyne Valley. These links are rare and geographically dispersed, yet there were even fewer references to western France. Perhaps it is more important that the early to mid-fourth millennium BC saw the development of accessible passage tombs in several parts of Atlantic Europe, including the

Iberian Peninsula where there was a particular emphasis on *circular mortuary monuments* in the north west (Fábregas Valcarce & Vilaseco Vázquez 2016). By this time, chambered tombs in Brittany and the west of France took a different form and were embellished in a different style.

A specific link may be even more revealing as there are radiocarbon dates from a series of *corbelled* passage graves in the west of Iberia. If the technique of construction recalls the architecture of important Irish monuments, it is revealing that their chronologies overlap. The dates for Spanish and Portuguese *tholos* tombs begin around 3500 BC and fall on either side of 3000 BC (Schulz Paulsson 2017: chapter 12). Another observation is most important. These architectural connections focus on the two main areas with Atlantic rock art and do not extend to the intervening region of western France where this way of building chamber tombs had been employed during an earlier phase. The fame of enormous Irish structures like Newgrange may have been a factor in linking distant areas.

Lastly, the adoption of Bell Beakers could be relevant as passage tombs were widely reused at that time. Activity continued in the Boyne Valley during the Late Neolithic and Chalcolithic periods (Carlin 2017). Connections along the coastline are indicated by the extraction and working of metals, and the dates for *tholos* tombs in western Iberia extend down to the mid third millennium BC. The evidence of ancient DNA suggests that they represent the first Atlantic network since the Early Neolithic period that might be related to the settlement of new people (Olalde et al. 2019).

LAXE DAS FERRADURAS, SPAIN

Laxe das Ferraduras is located by the entrance to an upland basin associated with a number of decorated outcrops (Peña Santos 1981). This example is exceptional as it features most of the main characteristics of the southern component of Atlantic Art (Fig. 14). The form of the rock is important too, as one group of images is on its upper surface, and the other on the steeply sloping side. Different motifs feature in these positions.

On top of the outcrop is a cup mark surrounded by three concentric rings. It is partly enclosed by another curving line which delimits a distribution of animal tracks, some of which lead towards – or away from – the circular motif. These are not horseshoes, as the name of the site suggest, and were the prints of cattle or, less probably, deer. Maybe the surface of the stone represented a real or imaginary landscape. Such associations are rare but are found elsewhere in north-west Iberia.

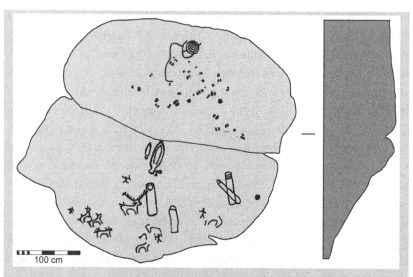

Fig. 14 The decorated rock at Laxe das Ferraduras, Spain, showing a circular design, animal tracks, daggers, idols and human figures. The profile of the rock is also illustrated. Information from Bradley (1997), Drawing: Aaron Watson

The flank of the outcrop features other elements that occur in Atlantic Art. In particular, there are drawings of two daggers (one twice the size of the other), a stag with prominent antlers, and four of the distinctive artefacts described as cylinder idols (one, and possibly two, of them with faces). The drawing of the stag impinges on one of these idols, while the positions of two objects of the same kind overlap. The surface of the rock is weathered, but there is no indication of a lengthy sequence. Around the limits of the panel are tiny human figures and animals. Another person shown in miniature is wielding the large dagger. It is common for drawings of weapons to be located on sloping or vertical surfaces (Fábregas Valcarce, Rodríguez Rellán & Rodríguez Álvarez 2011).

In this case, the drawings include two daggers of a type dating from the end of the third millennium BC (Fábregas Valcarce, Rodríguez Rellán & Rodríguez Álvarez 2011). The idols have obvious parallels in the Late Neolithic and Chalcolithic periods, especially in the south of Spain, and are dated between the mid fourth and late third millennia BC (Hurtado Perez 2008). Small quantities of Beaker pottery have been excavated at another decorated rock nearby (Seoane Veiga, Prieto Martínez & Dal Zovo 2013).

BEN LAWERS, SCOTLAND

The Ben Lawers estate overlooks one of the longest lochs in Scotland. The lower part of this mountain range divides into two zones, on either side of a wall built during the historical era to separate the area occupied throughout the year from summer pasture on the higher ground. Prehistoric monuments are restricted to the lower slopes, while the remains of post-medieval buildings occur further uphill (Atkinson 2016). There are exposures of rock in both areas. Petroglyphs are common and the most complex non-figurative designs tend to be at a greater elevation than the others.

Rock art is very common on the north side of Loch Tay where many sites command extensive views; pollen analysis shows that they were made in an open landscape (Bradley, Watson & Anderson-Whymark 2013: 52–6). The main concentration of petroglyphs overlooks the section of the loch that extends from north-east to south-west: the directions of the midsummer sunrise and midwinter sunset respectively (Figs. 15 and 16). Observers can watch the sun travelling across the sky above the opposite shore. In favourable conditions, the hills and valleys are reflected in the water, giving the illusion of an inverted world.

Fig. 15 Circular motifs overlooking Loch Tay on the mountainside at Ben Lawers, Scotland. The view is towards the north east. Photograph: Aaron Watson

Fig. 16 Circular motifs overlooking Loch Tay on the mountainside at Ben Lawers, Scotland. The view is towards the south west. Photograph: Aaron Watson

Two kinds of stone were selected for making the petroglyphs. They had quite different properties. Epidiorite was a hard rock and working it required some effort. Newly pecked designs would be emphasised by a glassy sheen. It was far easier to embellish mica schist, which has the distinctive property that it glitters in strong light; pecking the surface releases crystals with the same property. Excavation showed that both kinds of stone were chosen during prehistory and deposits of worked quartz accumulated around the panels. Some pieces were placed in fissures within the decorated surface.

Excavation found broken hammers which may have been used to make the petroglyphs. They clustered around the decorated rocks, but the number of broken pieces was not related to the hardness of the nearest stone; nor did it reflect the extent of the images or the work required to create them. Instead the distribution of these fragments focused on the exposures of mica schist. The simplest explanation is that not all the artefacts fractured in pecking the designs. Others were employed to pound the softer rock in order to make it glitter. Another possibility is that the crystals were collected and incorporated in pigment. In either case, the character of the stone was as important as the designs made on its surface (Bradley, Watson & Anderson-Whymark 2012: 60).

4 Alpine Rock Art: Unity and Diversity

Distributions and Datings

This is one of the best-known and most thoroughly documented styles in Europe and includes the World Heritage Site at Valcamonica (Fig. 17; de Marinis & Fossati 2012; Sansoni 2012). It is split between three countries – Italy, France and Switzerland – and has been studied in several different ways. There have been excavations in Italy and Switzerland, but not at Mont Bego in southern France. Stratified sequences have been investigated in monument complexes at Aosta, Sion and Valcamonica (Mezzena 1998; Gallay 2011; Poggiani Keller 2018), but until recently the rock art of Mont Bego was treated as one contemporary group (Huet 2017 and 2018). The petroglyphs of Mont Bego and Valcamonica have either been recorded in minute detail, or interpreted overambitiously in terms of Eurasian mythology (de Lumley 1995; Anati 1976) There are disagreements over dating, although superimposition is agreed to be important (de Saulieu 2004; Alexander 2009; Cassini & Fossati 2013; for more general accounts, see de Marinis, Dalmeri and Pedrotti (2012) and de Marinis (2013).

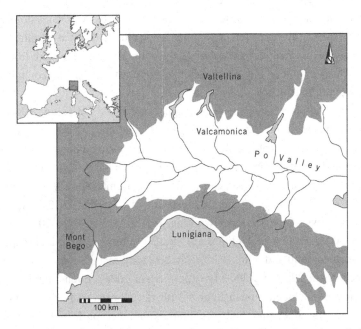

Fig. 17 The principal regions with rock art in the Alps and northern Italy. Information from de Saulieu (2004). Drawing: Aaron Watson

At the same time, these petroglyphs did not exist in isolation. Statue menhirs were important (Mezzena 1998; Poggiani Keller 2018), as well as their equivalents pecked into natural outcrops. They were shared with wider regions in the West Mediterranean, but, apart from those at Valcamonica, their distributions complement, or even avoid, those of petroglyphs (Robb 2009). The initial focus was on the images themselves. It is revealing that similar elements appear (with different authors) in both the *Oxford handbooks* on *the Neolithic* and *the Bronze Age* (Fossati 2015; de Saulieu 2013, respectively).

Panels of rock art are found in very different settings. The largest complexes were in valleys in the Central Alps and the Alpes Maritimes, but Valcamonica is in a domestic landscape, inhabited to the present day, and so is Valtellina. Related images have also been observed in the rock art of the Appennines (Cremonisi & Tosatti 2017). Mont Bego is upland pasture which is buried beneath snow for part of the year (de Lumley 1995). The important groups of statue stelae at Aosta and Sion are associated with routes leading through the Alps (Mezzena 1998; Gallay 2011), and those at Lunigiana were only 30 km or so from early copper mines in northern Italy. It is possible that evidence of metal extraction will also be found with concentrations of rock art and standing stones, as copper is available in some of the same areas (O'Brien 2015: chapter 5).

The visual repertoire varied between all these settings, and local chronologies did too. Thus the use of Mont Bego overlapped with activity at Valcamonica but extended over a shorter period (de Saulieu 2004; Huet 2017). On the other hand, Valcamonica reached its peak during the Late Bronze Age and Iron Age (Marretta 2013). It is not clear whether rock art was made continuously throughout this sequence.

Nor is it obvious when the first images were made (Marretta 2014). The oldest art has been attributed to the Upper Palaeolithic, while the metalwork portrayed in petroglyphs and on menhirs has been compared with well-documented examples in graves, whose own chronology has been analysed in detail. Important evidence comes from the Remedello cemetery on the edge of the Po Valley not far to the south (de Marinis 2013). There are different views of early copper working and its date (Dolfini 2013). In the Central Alps, the first petroglyphs are thought to represent the landscape and date between 3500 and 3000 BC. Stelae depicting metal artefacts were made between about 2900 and 2000 BC (de Saulieu 2004). Even-later images at Valcamonica included human figures with raised arms (*orantes*). They also feature spears rather than halberds, hunters mounted on horseback, inscriptions in Etruscan script, and drawings of diagnostic Iron Age artefacts (Marretta 2013).

The Variety of Images

If the superimpositions are correctly interpreted, the earlier panels of rock art include the abstract designs described as 'topographic representations' (Arcà 2000; Fossati 2002; Arcà 2013; Maretta 2018). These 'geometric' elements have been compared with megalithic art (Fossati 2015: 850) and the earliest have been dated to the second half of the fourth millennium BC (Casini & Fossati 2013). Stelae are also important, and both sculptures and petroglyphs are treated together here (Casini, de Marinis & Pedrotti 1995; Keates 2000; de Saulieu 2004). They feature drawings of weapons (daggers, halberds and axes), clothing and personal ornaments, scenes of farming, drawings of animals, and what are interpreted as solar motifs (Figs. 18 and 19). In common with the statues in other parts of the Central Mediterranean, these artefacts might be attached to a human body. That was normally the case with personal ornaments and weapons, but, unusually, at Valcamonica these images overlapped with the already-established repertoire of local rock art and look more like a display of trophies. There were further variations. Textiles like those on menhirs were apparently absent from Mont Bego; domesticated animals often featured at Mont Bego and Valcamonica; and wild animals were mostly depicted at Valcamonica. Most Chalcolithic sun symbols were around Valcamonica too, but, according to de Saulieu (2004), in the Early Bronze Age they also occurred at Mont Bego.

Fig. 18 Drawings of deer at Valcamonica, Italy. Photograph: Stephen Cogbill

Fig. 19 Stele depicting humans and animals at Valcamonica,
Italy. Photograph: Stephen Cogbill

The Contexts of the Images

Two relationships are especially important: between rock art and stelae; and
between the depictions of artefacts and finds of the same types in graves and
hoards. Both link the discussion to a wider area.

In northern Italy, the main concentrations of petroglyphs avoided the areas
with formal cemeteries, but there were single burials to their east and collective
burials to the west (Barfield 1986 and 2007: 453–7). Most of the menhirs are in
areas where single inhumations are uncommon, but their stereotyped appearance recalls that of a body in the grave. On the other hand, such stelae can be
associated with disarticulated bones which seem to have been treated as relics
(Poggiani Keller 2018). Both traditions are represented at Valcamonica, but the
distribution of actual daggers and halberds avoided the places where they were
shown on natural surfaces (Bianco Peroni 1994). There was a direct association
between menhirs and megalithic structures at Sion and Aosta (Mezzena 1998;
Gallay 2011; Armirotti, de Davide & Weeks 2018.), and more has been learnt by
excavations at Valcamonica (Fedele 2008 and 2013; Fedele & Fossati 2012;
Poggiani Keller 2018).

The repertoire varied both chronologically and between regions. In at least
two cases – Valcamonica and Mont Bego – it is clear that the earliest features

were non-figurative designs of kinds which also featured in later phases. On Mont Bego, they were overlain by drawings of horned figures (presumably cattle) and later by those of identifiable metalwork (Arcà 2013; Huet 2017). Where the images can be matched with weapon types, the earliest concentrations were at Valcamonica and Mont Bego. Those in the Alpine valleys north of Lake Garda were later in date, as were the decorated stelae at Lunigiana. Fewer images are assigned to the Bell Beaker phase and the Early Bronze Age when the main change was a reduction in the number of findspots on routes leading through the Alps (de Saulieu 2004). By the latter period, most of the information comes from Mont Bego and Valtellina, but at Valcamonica the sequence extended until the Iron Age with stone-walled settlements and drawings of buildings, distinctive artefacts, armed men and hunting scenes (Figs. 20 and 21; Bevan 2006; Marretta 2013).

The settings of Alpine rock art varied considerably. Here, there were two basic groups: those within the settled landscape, and examples in more isolated locations. The first group is illustrated by the Iron Age images at Valcamonica (Marretta 2013). By contrast, few artefacts of any kind are known from Mont Bego, which would have to be settled seasonally (Huet 2017). Here there are significant relationships between the rock art, the positions of upland lakes, and the paths followed by shepherds and their animals today. Others sites were positioned along the valley routes where stelae are commonest. In this context, they could be organised in

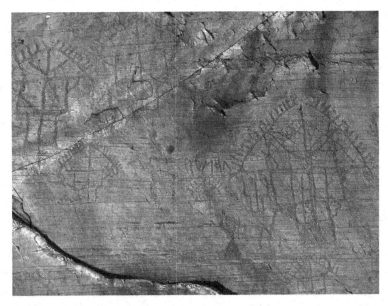

Fig. 20 Depictions of buildings at Valcamonia, Italy. Photograph: Cecilia dal Zovo

Fig. 21 Scene of combat at Valcamonia, Italy. Photograph: Cecilia dal Zovo

formal settings together with low stone platforms, cairns or tombs (Fedele 2008; Gallay 2011; Poggiani Keller 2018). Lines of anthropomorphic sculptures also occurred at Lunigiana south of the Alps (Pariboni et al. 2012).

The use of the pecked surfaces changed over time. The decorated rocks varied between *art discret* and *art monumentale*. These terms relate to the surfaces on which the designs were made: in one case, they were flat and inconspicuous; in the other, they were prominent and steep (de Saulieu 2004). Monumental art occupied dominant positions, but *art discret* was more difficult to find as it merged into the surrounding landscape. The most conspicuous images included human figures with weapons, ornaments and costumes and could be associated with wild animals and hunting scenes. These images could be replaced, modified or destroyed, often by superimposing other designs. *Art discret* showed weapons too, but newer panels were made beside the older ones, which were left intact. In this case, the artefacts were not associated with drawings of individual bodies, and domesticated animals featured in the same panels. Images identified as the sun appeared in both these groups.

There was a striking alternation between these treatments over time. There was monumental art in the Neolithic and also in the later Chalcolithic and Bell Beaker phases (de Saulieu 2004; Huet 2018). *Art discret* predominated early and again in the Bronze Age. *Art discret* was common at Valcamonica and Mont Bego. Monumental art was not important at the latter site, but was well represented at Valcamonica and on the routes crossing the Alps. The same is true at Lunigiana (Pariboni et al. 2012) where there were decorated stelae along the rivers that allowed communication from the west coast of Italy through the Appennines to the Po Valley. There were further depictions of weapons or armed figures until the Middle Bronze Age. Then there may have been a hiatus before the representations known as *orantes* at Valcamonica and the scenes of mounted warriors and hunters dated to the Iron Age.

The earlier phases have been investigated in most detail. The evidence from a few excavations emphasises the formal layout of the decorated stelae and their relationship with offerings and the remains of the dead. There were unusual deposits like the human teeth that seem to have been broadcast across a cultivated plot at Aosta, and there were also stone settings and cairns (Mezzena 1998). Alignments of stelae could be reworked and individual sculptures were damaged or rearranged (Gallay 2011). Older images were obliterated and replaced by new ones, especially in the Bell Beaker phase. The triangular platforms or cairns at these sites may echo the shape of the carved daggers, and another structure of this kind has been excavated at Arana in northern Italy where it is dated to the Chalcolithic period. A flat cemetery beside it dates from the Early Bronze Age (de Marinis & Valzolgher 2013: 53–8). Huet and Bianchi (2016) suggest that the same idea applies to the choice of pointed or triangular rocks for embellishment at Mont Bego.

Alpine Rock Art in Its Wider Context

Despite the similarities of style there was no unity of context. The earliest images may be the 'topographic representations'; then from 2900 BC they were supplemented by pictures of cattle, and eventually by scenes of cultivation (Arcà 2013). Drawings of diagnostic metalwork extended until about 2000 BC. There could have been a concern to claim, and even to sacralise, the landscape as it was first settled. That surely applies to Mont Bego where some of the images may have been made seasonally to represent the situation in home settlements some distance away. That may explain why plough teams were commonly depicted. Again there was an emphasis on the sun.

Not only did activity on Mont Bego start in the Neolithic, the earliest dated activity there followed the decline of axe production at Mont Viso not far to its north (Pétrequin et al. 2012; Pétrequin, Pétrequin & Gauthier 2017). Special trips into the mountains were already made during this period and may have established long-distance routes leading between the highlands and lowlands. People might have believed that these particular mountains were special. In fact, at Valcamonica, images were located within a landscape suitable for growing crops, but at Mont Bego they were made in a remote area where similar practices are not likely to have happened.

Copper is widely distributed in the Alps and its importance may be reflected by the contents of the rock art (O'Brien 2015: 68–75 and 117–23). At present there seems to be a striking relationship between copper sources north and south of the high ground and pivotal points along valley routes leading through the mountains. Here there were what Earle and his co-authors call 'bottlenecks' where its movement could have been controlled (Earle et al. 2015). These sites saw the erection of stelae, some of them associated with drawings of weapons. This applied to the north and north-western routes from the Po Valley. The same interpretation may extend to the Lunigiana complex which straddles important routes through the Apennines. New work has recognised a common metal pool extending from south to north across the Alps (Peruchetti et al. 2017).

There is a striking contrast between the early non-figurative designs and those depicting weapons and objects of adornment. They were shared by petroglyphs and statue stelae and illustrate a growing concern with personal status, expressed through portrayals of metal artefacts. Social position must have been important and these media provided ways of displaying it. The changing histories of these images may reflect the day-to-day politics of the Copper Age and Early Bronze Age. That may be why individual statues were so often remodelled or defaced and why some of them were levelled and destroyed. On the other hand, it was not until the Iron Age that the rock art of Valcamonica provides direct evidence of war bands and armed conflict. Although the same locations remained important for a long time, the concerns of the people who lived there were very different.

BUILDING A SEQUENCE AT MONT BEGO AND VALCAMONICA

Chronology has always posed a problem in the study of Alpine rock art. There have been two main difficulties. The first was that early researchers relied on subjective judgements. Thus human figures with their arms raised supposedly in prayer had been assigned to an early period of activity at Valcamonica simply because they were consistent with 'a Neolithic conception of society'; now it seems that they date from the Late Bronze Age (Fossati 2015: 858). There was never any evidence to support this peculiar idea, and in fact such motifs overlie drawings of diagnostic metalwork. Another assumption was that designs that were found together must have been made in the same period. This interpretation was favoured at Mont Bego but was not based on any evidence (Huet 2017).

In fact, several methods can be used to establish the histories of these sites. Perhaps the most secure is to analyse superimposed motifs, provided the diagnostic elements are represented sufficiently often. That is the commonest procedure and has provided consistent results at Valcamonica, Valtellina and Mont Bego (Arcà 2013; Huet 2017). The same method was employed at Valcamonica to show that that the human figures dated to the Iron Age were later than depictions of Bronze Age artefacts. Fragments of already-decorated stone – most of them from broken stelae – have also been discovered in excavations (Poggiani Keller 2018). In each case, 'topographic representations' occurred in earlier deposits than drawings of diagnostic metalwork. In turn, the ornaments and weapons represented in Alpine rock art resemble those in hoards and graves which can be dated by conventional methods.

Taken together, the results of these projects suggest that the earliest panels were Neolithic (Arcà 2013). The first drawings of daggers and halberds followed about 2900 BC, together with pairs of oxen (Fig. 22). This is later than the dates for the earliest knowledge of metallurgy in the region which is assigned to the mid fourth millennium BC (Dolfini 2013) and use-wear analysis on surviving artefacts indicates that halberds and

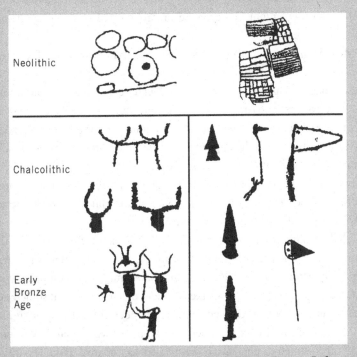

Fig. 22 The sequence of pecked motifs on Mont Bego, France. Information from Arcà (2013). Drawing: Aaron Watson

daggers played a largely ceremonial role and were seldom employed in combat (Dolfini 2011). The sequence extended down to 1200 BC when the production of images on Mont Bego came to an end. At Valcamonica, however, there was greatly increased activity towards the beginning of the Iron Age as completely new elements entered local rock art, in particular drawings of warriors, horsemen, hunters and buildings. The dating of these elements is supported by comparison with the designs on the bronze vessels known as *situlae*.

STATUE STELAE IN THE ALPS

The practice of erecting anthropomorphic statues was widely distributed across space and time. It extended from Eastern Europe to the Atlantic and from the Neolithic period to the Iron Age (Robb 2009). Stelae or statue menhirs took many different forms. Some were only roughly shaped to indicate shoulders and a head – that was particularly true in Brittany – while in other contexts faces were shown and the stones were equipped with costumes, ornaments and weapons. They had different histories, too. In the Neolithic period in western France and Iberia they might be complete or broken and could be built into passage graves.

Most examples in the Alps present a simple outline and not all of them are associated with distinctive artefacts, although the people who created these images might show occasional facial features or the outline of a distinctive costume (the textiles were considered by Harris in 2003). In other cases, bodies were equipped with ornaments and weapons of readily identifiable types, but the appearance of the sculptures seems essentially static. The organisation and clothing of the male statues may have been drawn from life, as they resemble the equipment of the 'Iceman' whose preserved body dates from the end of the fourth millennium BC (Robb 2009: 177–8). In the Central Mediterranean, the raising of statues ran in parallel with the creation of open-air rock art which featured most of the same elements. In each case, it was a feature of the Chalcolithic period and the Early Bronze Age. Here human bodies might be equipped with individual objects – perhaps an axe, a dagger or a halberd – but sometimes these artefacts were represented in greater numbers. On other sites, similar collections of metalwork were depicted on their own so that they resembled the distinctive deposits characterised as 'hoards' (Bradley 2017: chapter 5).

At the Petit Chasseur site, such stelae were erected in front of a megalithic tomb, but they were damaged and fragments were reused in a series of monumental cists during the Bell Beaker period (Mezzena 1998; Gallay 2011). While a few examples remained in position, many of those in the Alps were beheaded or pushed over (Gallay 2011; Poggiani Keller 2018). The distinctive outlines of the statues were also pecked on unshaped boulders or outcrops (Casini & de Marinis 2009; Casini & Fossati 2013). The relationship between these media is best evidenced at Valcamonica where the distributions of both traditions overlap.

Excavation has shown that these statues were originally organised in a line that has been described as a 'wall of ancestors' (Harrison & Heyd 2007: 163). Such files of human figures are documented at Sion, Aosta, Valcamonica and probably at Lunigiana (Gallay 2011; Pariboni et al. 2012; Poggiani Keller 2018). In these places, they could be associated with smaller stone settings, platforms and megalithic tombs, and with deposits of scattered human bones. At Valcamonica they were found with deposits of artefacts of the kind usually employed as grave goods (Poggiani Keller 2018). Many of the statues at Aosta and Sion were modified or damaged and were recycled as building material in the Copper Age. At Valcamonica, older statues provided a focus for another phase of activity in the Iron Age and Roman periods, after which they were destroyed (Fedele 2013 and 2015; Poggiani Keller 2018).

The principal 'sanctuaries' with settings of statue stelae were along valley routes leading through the high ground of the Alps and the Apennines. It is no coincidence that they feature so many depictions of metalwork. Copper and bronze daggers feature especially prominently, as they do in rock art. One of the most informative groups of sculptures comes from Lunigiana close to the west coast of the Italian peninsula (Pariboni et al. 2012). The male figures are clearly identified by their daggers, but the forms of the carved bodies of both men and women conform to a distinctive local style (Fig. 23). Their heads are half moon-shaped, their arms slope diagonally down the body, and their hands meet at the waist. The style of portrayal is distinctive, but it is even more striking that the entire composition resembles the form of a dagger. Its pommel echoes the unusual shape of the head, and the outline of the blade echoes the angular configuration of the arms. It seems as if the people represented at Lunigiana – both women and men – were equated with the daggers represented on the stone. Or was it the weapons that were treated as living

Fig. 23 Statue of a person armed with a dagger at Taponecco,
northern Italy. Photograph: Stephen Cogbill

beings? In any event, the statue stelae were located on the routes through
the mountains along which metal artefacts might have been travelled.

5 Rock Art in Northern Europe: Facing Two Ways

Here there are two supposedly separate and successive styles, once named after
hunters and farmers respectively, although that terminology is no longer used
(Malmer 1981; Goldhahn & Ling 2013; Goldhahn 2018). Their distributions
differ, and variants of the Northern style are not confined to Scandinavia but
extend to Finland and Russia. Even the Southern style is represented in north
Germany (Capelle 2008). In some ways, both groups are still studied according
to modern national boundaries and languages (Nimura 2016).

The Northern Style

The Northern style featured wild animals, sea creatures, hunting scenes and
boats, but different species dominated each major complex (Gjerde 2010;
Sognnes 2017). This is unlikely to be evidence of economic specialisation
and could imply a kind of totemism – Fugelstvedt (2017) suggests an even

earlier phase of animism. There is evidence of composites – elk-boats and therianthropes – and shape shifting seems to have been important (Herva & Lahelma 2019: 70–3 and 114–17). Despite these 'mythological' elements, there was a degree of three-dimensional realism in the drawings themselves. Both Helskog (2014) and Gjerde (2010) have identified 'micro-landscapes' in Norway and Russia. The character of the rock was most important. Among its most striking features were quartz veins, stream channels, pools and glacial striations. In Northern Scandinavia, images were made beside cataracts where the high level of sound could have had psychoactive properties (Goldhahn 2002). On the other hand, in Finland there was a preference for anthropo-morphic outcrops and natural portals, and here handprints picked out in red pigment suggest that it was important for people to touch the rock (Lahelma 2008).

There was a special emphasis on the seashore, riverbanks, waterfalls and small islands. Most of the images were pecked, but there is evidence of paintings extending from the Arctic as far south as Gothenburg (Schultz Paulsson, Isendahl & Frykman Markurth 2019). A deposit of red ochre has been found in an excavated settlement close to the petroglyphs at Nämforsen (Goldhahn 2010: fig. 8.6). All the Finnish rock art was painted, apart from undated cup marks (Saksa, Bel'skiy & Mizin 2017). In Norway, domestic features including dwellings are found nearby – for example, at Vingen and Alta (Lødøen & Mandt 2012a; Helskog 2014).

Chronology poses a particular problem. The Northern style cannot have existed until the ice caps had melted. There are three main issues:

> The animals that feature in this style of rock art are also represented by small portable artefacts which date from the Mesolithic period.
> There are sites where the imagery is overlain by diagnostic Bronze Age elements or where they occur together on the same rocks (Wrigglesworth 2006; Bertilsson 2018). On the other hand, there are a few Bronze Age images elsewhere in the north, located within pockets of fertile land close to the sea (Kaul 2014). Here only one style is represented.
> There are possible links with elements of Sámi belief recorded in the historical era – the use of drums, and the ritual importance of the bear (Helskog 2012 and 2014). Even if this style of rock art had a finite currency, it may have expressed a remarkably resilient view of the world.

Coastal sites have a special significance because of land uplift. As sea levels fell during the postglacial period, newly exposed rocks became available. Provided they were made at the water's edge, the images on their surface can be placed in chronological order. The method seems to work, but, strictly speaking, it provides a *terminus post quem*. At Alta in Arctic Norway, Helskog has identified six phases, beginning about 5000 BC and ending around AD 100 (Helskog 2014: 28–9). Gjerde (2010) favours a similar scheme but identifies five phases extending between 5200 BC and AD 200. Why was the seashore so significant? Were these surfaces the first to be exposed after winter snow? Were they chosen because the rock was free of lichen? Were the images made there to prevent the sea from retreating (Nimura 2016)? Helskog (1999) argues that the major complexes were located where three levels of the cosmos – the land, the sky and the sea – all came together. Again the case is strengthened by analogy with local beliefs (Herva & Ylimmaunu 2014). The largest groups of rock art are interpreted as aggregation sites. One example at Vingen has been recorded in exceptional detail (Lødøen & Mandt 2012a). The Northern style is linked with widely distributed circumpolar imagery, important elements of which include depictions of boats and the sun (Lahelma 2017). Their presence is understandable in areas where travel would be by water and the sun could not be seen for part of the year.

The Southern Style

All the surviving images in this tradition were pecked, but pieces of red burnt clay are often found in excavation, raising the possibility that they were a source of pigment (Bengtsson & Ling 2008). If so, no sign of painting survives. In contrast to the Northern tradition, this style is treated as specifically Scandinavian, but has been studied rather differently in Norway from Sweden and Denmark. It is often compared with concepts and imagery found in areas as far away as Central Europe, the Mediterranean, Mesopotamia and Egypt. The case is plausible because of occasional long-distance imports of glass beads and metalwork, and the export of Baltic amber (Kaul 2017). The contents of South Scandinavian art vary regionally and even by medium. Thus there are petroglyphs in most areas, but stone ship settings are common on the island of Gotland where rock carvings are almost absent (Wehlin 2013). The evidence from the Bjare peninsula in south-west Sweden is dominated by cup marks (Nord 2009) and there are concentrations of life-size footprints in central Norway (Sognnes 2001: 69–71). Towards the south, pictures of ships, horses and the sun are shared between metalwork and rock art (Kaul 1998: 265–9). That connection is useful for their interpretation, but also as dating evidence. Thus the images identified in rock art are fixed by reference to decorated bronzes from the Early to the Late Bronze Age. The main subjects of the petroglyphs are watercraft (of several different types, a few with improbably large crews), people, animals, hunting, fighting, weapons and tools (Figs. 24 and 25). There was an obvious emphasis on masculinity among the later figures

Fig. 24 Humans, animals and boats and Rickeby, Sweden.
Figs. 24 - 27 show pecked images which have been painted to display
them to the public. Photograph: Courtney Nimura

Fig. 25 Boats with their crews at Hornnes, Norway. Photograph: Courtney Nimura

Fig. 26 A wheel cross and a possible solar image at Evenstorp,
Sweden. Photograph: Courtney Nimura

(Coles 2005, 31–52). There are also wheel crosses interpreted as solar images,
ploughs, and footprints or foot soles (depending on whether people were
wearing shoes). The earlier imagery follows both the Baltic and the Atlantic,
but the west coast assumed more importance during the Late Bronze Age and
earliest Iron Age (Coles 2000 and 2005; Ling 2013 and 2014; Nimura,
Skoglund & Bradley 2020).

The inland art of southern Sweden resembles the petroglyphs of Denmark
(Glob 1969). In coastal areas, a common theme is the daily movement of the sun
which is drawn by a horse across the sky (Fig. 26). At night, it travels underwater carried on a ship (Kaul 1998). These beliefs must have been widely shared
and the sun is associated with horses and boats throughout Indo-European
poetry and myth (West 2007; Kristiansen 2012). This was not a new development as the solar barque had been an important concept in Egypt since the third
millennium BC.

In Scandinavia, there was considerable local variation. Depictions of weapons, whether Early or Late Bronze Age, are not found everywhere, although
they can easily dominate the discussion. In Bohuslän, outsize human figures
may be on higher ground and superimposed on older images (Ling 2014: 146).
Everywhere the clearest association is between ships, watercourses and the sea
(Nimura 2016). These elements can also be associated with people, animals and
wheel crosses. By contrast, very few ship carvings occur far inland except

beside major lakes with connections to the ocean. Otherwise, the inland rock art is largely made up of cup marks and footprints (Skoglund 2006; Nord 2009). Circular motifs are also found, plus occasional drawings of wheeled vehicles (Fig. 27)

The coastal concentrations on the Baltic and Atlantic tend to be by sheltered moorings about half a day's travel apart (Ling 2014: 223), but there are many exceptions. There was an emphasis on river mouths accessing the interior, with drawings of ships where they entered two huge inland lakes (Nimura, Sloglund & Bradley 2020). Rock art was also associated with a few coastal or near-coastal cairns. In fact there was an association between other cairns and rock art for it can even underlie them, and in the west of Norway both are found together close to the water's edge (Wrigglesworth 2015). Here the graves contain pebbles and shells collected from the beach (cf. Nordenborg Myhre 2004: 218). Maritime images are mixed with inland motifs at large sites close to where rivers enter Lake Vänern. Unlike the drawings of ships at the water's edge, they are set back from the shoreline (Nimura, Skoglund & Bradley 2020). These places might have been where local communities dealt with strangers.

There are two main approaches to chronology. One is direct comparison with the decorated metalwork – weapons, ornaments and especially razors. The typological sequence of ships is based on the images on well-dated artefacts (Kaul 1998). At the larger sites, existing motifs could be enhanced and recut

Fig. 27 A boat with its crew at Husaby, Sweden, together with a wheel cross and a foot sole. Photograph: Richard Bradley

(Hauptmann Wahlgren 2002) and it seems possible that certain drawings of watercraft were updated to conform to a newer style (Milstreu 2017). Another source of information is the wooden boat found in a waterlogged deposit at Hjortspring in Denmark, the remains of which date from the pre-Roman Iron Age (Crumlin-Pedersen & Trakadas 2003); other fragments of similar date have been found in Arctic Norway (Wickler 2019). Shoreline displacement is important too, although its extent varied from one region to another (Ling 2014). Again, the assumption is that newly exposed surfaces were carved as soon as they became available. The two kinds of dating evidence provide similar results.

Another approach is favoured, especially in Norway (Nordenborg Myhre 2004). Here the classification of ships suggests some continuity between boats depicted in the 'Mesolithic' Northern style and the earliest vessels attributed to the (Bronze Age) Southern style (Gjerde 2017). Was this where the latter tradition first developed (Sognnes 2001; Melheim & Ling 2017)? It is the area where Neolithic farming faltered or lapsed until the end of the third millennium BC (Nielsen, Persson & Solheim 2019). This could help to explain why certain elements were shared between both traditions: the strict adherence to the coast and the water's edge; the overwhelming emphasis on boats; drawings suggesting shape-shifting and transformation scenes; and the incorporation of cracks, quartz veins and watercourses in the compositions (Fahlander 2013). As in the Northern tradition, there seems to be evidence of a three-tier cosmology (Helskog 1999; Bradley 2009: 162–8). Even the supposedly Mediterranean elements in Scandinavian rock art can be explained, especially the link between vessels and the sun which is documented throughout the Arctic (Lahelma 2017).

It is harder to contextualise these developments in relation to wider processes (Goldhahn 2014; Skoglund, Ling & Bertilsson 2017). There were the references to the sun in Northern rock art – whatever its date – but in Germany they extended to the Nebra Sky Disc and the Wismar Horn in the Early Bronze Age (Kristiansen & Larsson 2005: 195–6). During the same period, Baltic amber was especially prized in Central Europe (Vandkilde 2017). It was the same colour as the sun and had the unusual property of retaining heat. More important, like the sun itself, it emerged from beneath the sea (Herva & Lahelma 2019, 156–62).

Contacts with more distant areas increased during the Urnfield period as decorated metalwork started to replace petroglyphs in Denmark and the south of Sweden. Here there was still an association between the sun, horses, boats and the dead, for the decorated razors are commonly found in graves. Perhaps there were two ways of transmitting specialised knowledge, directed to different audiences in different regions: small razors with drawings that could only have communicated to the individual; and decorated outcrops where the rock art was addressed to large gatherings (Bradley 2015). Fire was important at the latter sites, as were deposits of quartz. More artefacts were deposited at cup-marked rocks than at complex panels which may have been comparatively isolated (Bengtsson & Ling 2008; Petersson & Toreld 2015, 85–146).

All South Scandinavian metalwork was foreign or reworked and there is no evidence for the use of local ores (Ling et al. 2013). That also applies to the kinds of object depicted in rock art – both Early and Late Bronze Age – and these pictures were a special feature of sheltered landing places on the shore. Warriors, scenes of conflict and pictures of abnormally large boats even suggest the existence of 'seafaring chiefdoms' on the west coast of Scandinavia controlling the import of metal at a time when less was available (Ling & Uhnér 2014; Ling, Earle & Kristiansen 2018). These scenes account for only part of the distribution of rock art, but, where they are present, long-distance maritime expeditions could have taken place (Ling & Cornell 2017; Horn 2018). A similar idea was proposed by Randsborg who related the Viking raids of the ninth century AD to a similar reduction in the supply of silver (Randsborg 1980: chapter 7).

In contrast to the drawings of watercraft, the petroglyphs away from the coast emphasised cup marks, footprints (and wheel crosses in some areas). The drawings of feet faced the solar arc or the positions of the solstices and were often organised in pairs, as if to indicate where participants should stand during particular events (Fig. 28; Skoglund, Nimura & Bradley 2017). On certain sites, they were so small that they may have belonged to children

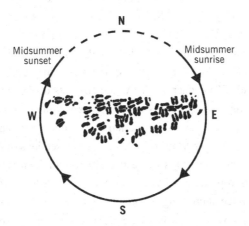

Fig. 28 Pairs of pecked footprints at Faglum, Sweden, showing their orientations and the position of the sun during the course of a year. Information from Burrenhult (1973). Drawing: Aaron Watson

(Hauptmann Wahlgren 2002). Was solar imagery of these kinds combined with notions of the south as a source of shining metal? Sun discs were made out of bronze or gold and were shown conveyed on vehicles drawn by a horse. Their equivalents seem to have been carried on board ships. Whichever material was used, these discs were lavishly decorated and would have caught the light. Did the depictions of the sun come to symbolise the new materials? If so, then elements of a long-standing cosmology might have been reinterpreted in local terms. It may be no accident that in the Early Bronze Age people at Järrestad in Scania could have watched the midwinter sunrise over the Baltic, their positions marked by footprints pecked into the surface of the rock (Skoglund, Nimura & Bradley 2017). The site was located not far from the coast where foreign metalwork dating from to the same period was depicted by the water's edge (Skoglund 2016: 66–77).

North European Rock Art in Its Wider Context

The distinctiveness of this region is shown by its unusual combination of two systems of belief at a time when geographical axes were changing. The most important was the shift from North to South Scandinavian rock art, which may have been precipitated by the expansion of agriculture and its adoption in new areas. The north must always have been a source of furs, but in the Bell Beaker phase imported metal became equally significant. Some could have been carried across the Gulf of Bothnia, but to an increasing extent it came from Central Europe and even further afield. It seems as if amber travelled in the opposite direction (Kaul 2017). These processes have been known for a long time, but current research suggests that they are illustrated by rock art and the places where it was made. What ensued was a new accommodation between long-standing beliefs among people in the North and those in South Scandinavia who established close relationships with communities in Central and Western Europe (Vandkilde 2017: chapter 5). As the contents of the art suggest, travel by sea was all-important. So was access to exotic raw materials, including metalwork from as far away as the Iberian Peninsula. It may have encouraged extended voyages – even periods of warfare – along sections of the coast (Ling, Earle & Kristiansen 2018). This was especially true in the first millennium BC when Northern Europe was at the farthest limit of the Atlantic Bronze Age and may account for the increasing amount of rock art along the west coast of Sweden and Norway. It is hardly surprising that these processes lost much of their importance when the supply of foreign metal diminished in the Early Iron Age.

SUPERIMPOSED IMAGES AT BARDAL, NORWAY

At Bardal in central Norway, typical features of the Northern and Southern traditions are found on the same rock and many of the images were superimposed (Gjessing 1935 and 1936; Sognnes 2008). This is unusual but not unique. It is clear that the images in the Northern tradition are more weathered than the others, but it seems possible that both groups of drawings spanned considerable periods of time. The drawings of wild animals were executed in more than one style, while the depictions of boats that overlie them started early in the Bronze Age (Fig. 29). The latest examples date from the Iron Age. Despite this lengthy sequence it is uncertain why the pictures were superimposed. Was it an act of iconoclasm, or did this place have a long-established significance, in which case

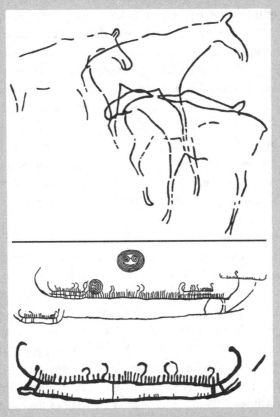

Fig. 29 Superimposed motifs at Bardal, Norway. Elk are shown in the upper part of the figure, and Bronze Age boats with members of their crew in the lower part. Information from Gjessing (1935 and 1936) and Sognnes (2008). Drawing: Aaron Watson

its reuse might have been intended as a reference to the past (Wrigglesworth 2006)?

The rock is unusually large and its shape has been compared with the body of a whale: one of the creatures portrayed at the site. The surface of the stone may also have attracted attention, for it is characterised by a series of lenticular hollows resembling eyes. They are especially striking because their outlines were emphasised by veins of quartz. The rock had another unusual property, for water emerges from its surface for a long time after rain. For people in the past, this stone could have possessed special powers.

The first images were outline drawings of elk, some of them more than life size. The positions of these creatures overlap one another and Sognnes (2017) suggests that this was done to portray a herd of animals. The single depiction of the whale is no less than 4.6 m long. The presence of land mammals and a creature associated with the sea in the same group of petroglyphs emphasises the importance of the shoreline. It is no accident that the earliest images at Bardal were located near the water.

The situation changed as the land rose and the coast retreated during the second and first millennia BC, but the same surface was used for drawings in the South Scandinavian style. This relationship could not have happened by chance as the densest distribution of Bronze Age boats was superimposed on the pictures of animals made during earlier phases; although the later petroglyphs extend into an area that had not been used before, the most striking images in both styles are in exactly the same location.

The later drawings feature much of the repertoire of the Southern tradition. There are large seagoing vessels together with their crews as well as smaller watercraft, some of which are apparently empty. Those on board one of the largest boats may be playing the kind of bronze trumpet called a lur. Two other people are shown standing on dry land. One seems to be wearing a horned helmet, and both have the enlarged calves that typify human figures in Bohuslän. The other motifs also have wider parallels. Above the boats are curvilinear motifs interpreted as drawings of the sun, and scattered across the decorated surface there are pairs of footprints. Although Bardal is located on the edge of their distribution, they resemble motifs that are common further to the south.

Lastly, towards the edges of the panel there are drawings of boats of the kind dated to the Iron Age. Here they are found together with depictions of horses, which became a significant feature of Scandinavian rock art in its latest phase. Although weapons are absent, the rock art of Bardal encapsulates many of the most widely represented elements in North European rock art.

KLINTA – SCANDINAVIAN SOLAR COSMOLOGY

This decorated stone from Klinta was recovered a hundred years ago from the site of a burial mound on the Baltic island of Öland. It depicts horses, ships, and a circular motif defined by a cup mark enclosed by three concentric rings. There are other cup marks close to this design, and more are pecked into three sides of the stone. Although it has been considered as part of a cist, its distinctive form suggests that it was a menhir, more than a metre high.

The full significance of this discovery was not apparent as the images were originally traced on transparent film and published in mirror image (Burenhult 1973: 66). That would not have seemed significant at the time, but the more recent work of Kaul (1998) has emphasised the importance of horses and boats in relation to Bronze Age cosmology. The direction in which they are travelling has become a significant feature (Fig. 30). The

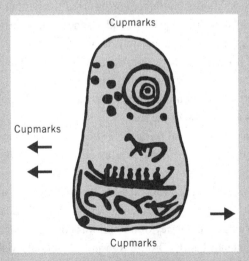

Fig. 30 The decorated stone from Klinta, Sweden, showing a possible solar motif, the distribution of cup marks, and the directions in which horses and boats are travelling across the decorated surface. (The cup marks extend to the underside of the stone but would not have been visible when it was standing). Information from Bradley (2009). Drawing: Aaron Watson

concentric rings are thought to represent the sun, and the decorated metalwork studied by Kaul seems to illustrate its movement over a twenty-four-hour cycle. During the hours of daylight it could be observed crossing the sky from left to right before it set in the west. But by the following morning it had returned to its starting point and rose above the eastern horizon. What had happened during the hours of darkness? Kaul's reading of the imagery engraved on Bronze Age metalwork involves a complex cycle. During the hours of daylight the sun was drawn across the sky, usually by a horse. At night it was carried underwater on a ship. It would return to its original position unseen by human eyes. The differences between day and night are illustrated by the direction of travel: from left to right between sunrise and sunset, and from right to left during the night.

That is why it is important to record the petroglyphs from Klinta correctly. The drawings are organised in two layers, one above the other. The lower level features two ships, one empty and the other with its crew. The empty boat travels from left to right, but the vessel drawn above it moves in the opposite direction. It is of Early Bronze Age type and contains at least seven people (the total is more likely to be fourteen as each image could show a pair of individuals seated opposite one another). Similarly, two, and possibly three, horses cross the bottom of the panel moving towards the right, while another one returns in the opposite direction. It is depicted immediately above a vessel that follows the same course. It may be that these images, with their emphasis on horses and ships stand for the day and night respectively, and that could be why the upper part of the stone features a circular design which is usually interpreted as a depiction of the sun.

The panel has two unusual features: the horses and boats travel together in both directions, and the stone was associated with a burial mound. These features have still to be explained, but some of the same elements appear on the kerb of a well-excavated round barrow at Sagaholm (Goldhahn 2016) and in the burial chamber at Kivik (Goldhahn 2013). It seems possible that the journey of the sun was compared with the human life course. That may be why Bronze Age and later burials were associated with stone settings in the form of a ship.

Less is said about the cup marks on three sides of the stone from Klinta. They occur on top of the decorated panel and continue down its left hand edge. They also extend across its base, which is weathered as if it had been set in the ground. A second group of cup marks is associated with the circular motif in the main panel. They follow almost the same configuration and are represented on three sides of this image but are absent to its right. Their appearance and disappearance is similar to the behaviour of the sun in Kaul's interpretation of the drawings on Bronze Age metalwork.

Finally, comparable elements can be identified at other sites in the Southern tradition, but one feature is common to many of them. They were located beside, or very close to, the shoreline in places where the sun could be viewed rising from the sea or setting into the water. Its appearance might have been compared with that of imported metalwork which carried similar designs to the petroglyphs and was buried with the dead. It was no accident that the findspot at Klinta was so near to the Baltic. Maybe the mound was one of the places from which people journeyed to the domain of the dead.

6 Comparisons

How did I come to investigate prehistoric rock art? There were some pragmatic considerations – the process is non-destructive, and need not involve expensive specialist analyses – but in Britain (which was my concern at the time), the main reason was that it provided a link between the imagery associated with Neolithic artefacts or monuments, and places in the wider landscape. That was particularly important since so little was known about the settlement pattern of the period. At the same time, it seemed important to assess the claim that British and Irish rock art was closely allied with that in north-west Iberia (Bradley 1997: 41–8 and 201–15). Once a project to investigate that question was under way another challenge presented itself. How was the southern expression of Atlantic rock art in Galicia and Portugal related to Schematic Art which extended over the remaining parts of the Iberian Peninsula (Bradley & Fábregas Valcarce 1996)?

Much of this work concerned the non-figurative imagery shared between rock art and other media. How did it compare with those traditions in which at least the outer meanings of the drawings could be recognised (Bradley 2009)? In Bronze Age Scandinavia, boats were seagoing vessels even if they carried the sun; footprints marked the stances of people or other beings that, for whatever reason, might have stood on the rock. Again I became interested in the relationship between painted or pecked motifs and similar images in other media: on decorated metalwork, on the structures in which the dead were buried; and in places where the same types of metalwork were deposited.

In every case, the lesson was the same. There was little to be gained from studying rock art in isolation or even from treating it as a specialised field of research. Might it be investigated more productively by relating its creation to broader processes in prehistoric society? There were some excellent models to follow. The final section sketches my first impressions and outlines a number of themes that can be addressed in future research.

Common Concerns

In principle, there is no reason why the same elements should be shared between the styles of rock art documented in different parts of Europe. The question of direct contacts is well worth studying, but it may be equally important that these local developments illustrate common concerns. In several regions, the archaeological sequence seems to have moved in similar directions, although this did not necessarily happen simultaneously (Robb in press). In fact, it is remarkable how far the rock art of separate areas appears to illustrate the same features.

The first concerns the connection between rock art and the adoption of agriculture. The relationship between the subsistence economy and ancient visual culture is clearly illustrated in two regions which are unlikely to have had any contact with one another. Although there are unresolved problems of chronology in both areas, the same duality can be seen towards opposite ends of Europe. To the south, it is documented by the puzzling relationship between Levantine Art, Macroschematic Art, and Schematic Art. To the north, the same problems arise with the relationship between the styles formerly described as hunters' art and farmers' art respectively. In the Iberian Peninsula it is obvious that such traditions overlapped, although it is not clear when or why the style that depicts wild animals and hunting scenes originated. In this case, it seems possible that certain images were intended as a commentary on the other elements during a phase when settlement by immigrant farmers impinged on the territories occupied by indigenous people. Here an apt comparison is with contact-period art in other parts of the world.

The problem is quite different in Fennoscandia, for here there is no agreement when the Northern Style of rock art went out of use. It seems to share elements with the ethnography of the post-medieval period, meaning that the belief system to which it referred might have outlasted the practice of painting and carving surfaces in the landscape. The Southern style, on the other hand, does include certain of the same elements but it combines them with features associated with farming, seafaring and the introduction of metalwork. As in Spain, components of these two traditions can be superimposed on the same panels or may respect one another, but, in this case, such situations are rare and there is nothing to show how long an interval was involved.

Where there is convincing evidence of superimposition, comparable sequences have been recognised, although their wider significance has seldom been discussed. In the Alps, for instance, the geometric designs sometimes described as 'topographic representations', are among the oldest elements, although some were still being made during later phases (Casini & de Marinis 2009). On Mont Bego, the first examples predate the drawings of horned figures, including pairs of oxen, which are clearly related to early land use. Similarly, non-figurative designs also predominate in Atlantic rock art where again they are attributed to its earliest stage. Comparable scenes referring to hunting and the sea are shown in the first monumental art of western France (Cassen 2009), but it is uncertain whether it also features domesticates (Scarre 2011, 85–6). Some designs are believed to refer to the local topography – the Alpine examples have been compared with maps, and their Iberian counterparts show the tracks of people and animals. The circular motifs are closely associated with drawings of deer which seem to be entering or leaving them. Although there is a risk of imposing post-Renaissance visions of landscape on the prehistoric evidence, there does seem to have been a new concern with the definition of territory and routes across the terrain. Whatever the correct interpretation, it is clear that the wider associations of these images do not suggest a practical explanation. In the Alps, there seem to be drawings of plough teams working in what was obviously an unsuitable environment. In Britain and Ireland, the same kinds of design were applied to outcrops in the open landscape, standing stones and chambered tombs. As the land was settled, certain locations may have been thought of as special. The point is made in an account of the first post-glacial art in Northern Europe:

> To move into a new and unknown landscape would mean to negotiate with the unknown powers in the area. A gradual ritual appropriation of the land must be made. In the earliest phase after the deglaciation numerous phenomena occurred that made the landscape dangerous and unpredictable . . . . The earliest rock carvings in the area are seen as places where rituals of appropriation were performed. (Forsberg 2006: 101)

In fact, early rock art in several regions of Europe illustrates a similar sense of place and a preference for the same kinds of features. Such sites might be comparatively accessible, but there were others on, or even beyond, the edges of the settled landscape. They might be in secluded locations connected with passes and routes through mountainous terrain. In many instances, the characteristics of the rock itself were important. Several elements were widely shared, although this need not imply any direct connection between those regions.

Distinctive landmarks were referenced by the placing of rock art and it is likely that they enjoyed a special significance before any images were made there – that was probably the case in Southern Africa where ethnographic evidence is available (Deacon 2001). Examples in prehistoric Europe include the selection of mountains and rock outcrops that resemble the human form, a predilection for extended views over the land and sea, the choice of narrow ledges in upland settings, and even the proximity of waterfalls. In every tradition it was the properties of the rock that attracted attention. Such features included the colour of the stone, the presence of mineral veins and inclusions of quartz, and the location of panels where the images would be refreshed by flowing water. In Iberia, it is clear that cliffs and rock shelters were painted at points with unusual acoustic properties. Sounds might be amplified and echo off the rock face. The same happened in North European rock art (Rainio et al. 2018). Different writers have suggested that panels of rock in Iberia, the Alps and Scandinavia commanded views of the solstices (Mauro Mijares 2010; Fernández Quintano 2013; García Quintela & Santos Estévez 2015; Versaci 2019). In Britain and Ireland, circular motifs in the Atlantic tradition are associated with radial lines which are generally directed towards the east: the direction of the rising sun. In Galicia, similar motifs are orientated towards the south where the sun is at its height (Bradley 1997: tables 9 and 29). Lines of stelae in the Alps also have solar alignments (Harrison & Heyd 2007). A similar idea extends to the orientation of footprints in the petroglyphs of South Scandinavia (Skoglund, Nimura & Bradley 2017) and the paintings of the sun in Iberian Schematic Art (Versaci 2019).

These examples share a feature that has played an increasing role in recent studies. They suggest that the rock was treated as a living being and that the processes which took place there account for its special significance (Jones 2017; Fahlander 2019; Goldhahn 2019b: chapter 8; Herva & Lahelma 2019: chapter 2). Perhaps there was no conceptual distinction between the bands of white quartz incorporated in the panels and the surface of the sea (Bradley et al. 2003). Similarly, the drawings of ships in Scandinavian rock art were animated where they were crossed by running water (Bradley 2009: 197–8 and 208). Such cases suggest a role for a more symmetrical archaeology, but, in most instances, its success will depend on analogy with ethnographic examples. This seems possible in northern Norway, Finland and Russia (Lahelma 2008; Gjerde 2010; Helskog 2014; Lahelma 2017).

Such sites emphasise the relationship between the rocks selected for embellishment – their forms, locations and the processes affecting them – and the distinctive images that were created there. A notable feature of several regional traditions is that these motifs could be overlain by representations of distinctive kinds of artefacts, particularly weapons made of copper and bronze. This represents a significant development in the archaeology of different areas, but it was by no means synchronous. For example, it may have happened in the Alps before it did in Atlantic Europe.

One point of departure for subsequent developments was the embellishment of freestanding monoliths whose shapes evoked the human form. They have been described by a variety of terms – statue menhirs, stelae, standing stones – and were widely distributed (Robb 2009 and 2015). Again, it is uncertain how far different regional groups were related to one another, but the images associated with them show an unusual degree of overlap with the open-air rock art of Valcamonica. This was not the only place where statues were associated with features that were also drawn on outcrops; other examples occur in Schematic Art, and occasionally in Atlantic Art. In some regions they lacked such obvious counterparts in the open air. The most striking evidence comes from the passage graves of north-west France (Cassen 2009), but in inland parts of the same country, human figures with similar attributes were depicted on prominent rocks as well as statues (Pétrequin, Pétrequin & Gauthier 2017: 761–845).

Such stelae had an extended currency. The special importance of Neolithic standing stones has been acknowledged in recent studies as it has become clear how many of the decorated pieces built into tombs had originally stood in the open air. Some were introduced to the monuments without any modification, but others were reworked or broken when it happened. This evidence is familiar in Brittany where other decorated menhirs remain *in situ* (Cassen 2009). More recently, the same phenomenon has been studied in Spain and Portugal (Bueno Ramírez, Balbín Behrmann & Barroso Bermejo 2007; Bueno Ramírez, Balbín Behrmann & Barroso Bermejo 2012; Bueno Ramírez et al. 2016). Just as these sculptures might be modified when they were reused, it has become clear that their counterparts in the wider landscape could be changed. The clearest examples of this process were the treatment of Chalcolithic stelae in Alpine valleys (Gallay 2011; Poggiani Keller 2018). In the Late Bronze Age, the same applied to the statues of south-western Iberia (Harrison 2004: 46–52; Díaz-Guardamino 2010 and 2014).

Since similar processes were followed at different times, there are dangers in comparing them too directly. They could have originated independently. On the other hand, they did share certain features with one another and also with open-air rock art. In most cases the human body was represented quite schematically, but according to local conventions. Certain examples provided little more than a frame for a display of special artefacts. They included jadeitite axes in the Neolithic period in Brittany (Pétrequin et al. 2012: 918–45), as well as weapons and ornaments in the Chalcolithic and Early Bronze Age phases at Valcamonica. They were equivalent to the distinctive material found in votive deposits, graves and hoards (Bradley 2017: 86–96). The same types could be represented on their own, as happened in the Alps, Atlantic Europe and South Scandinavia. A similar sequence is described by García Sanjuan (1999: fig. 11) in his account of the stelae in south-west Iberia.

If those stone sculptures provided a *frame* for a display of artefacts – in certain cases more items than any one person might have worn – the character of those objects is worth discussing here. Although there are many exceptions, two features are particularly revealing. Some of those tools, weapons and ornaments must have been obtained from distant sources. Examples include the displays of Alpine axes that feature on tombs and menhirs in Brittany, the drawings of unhafted axeheads represented on the west coast of Scotland, and the panoply of bronze weapons that features in South Scandinavian rock art. Decorated stelae could play an important role in long-distance relationships. Those in Northern Italy include a major concentration not far from early copper mines, while similar groups of armed figures are found at strategic points on routes through the Alps. They were probably located along the paths by which metalwork was taken between Italy, Switzerland and Austria. Similarly, coastal outcrops on the Baltic and Atlantic coasts of Scandinavia depict weapons from Central Europe and probably from other regions. In this case, stelae do not occur, but these panels are often in places where people could land their boats after a lengthy voyage, or they line narrow channels where the movement of travellers, objects and raw materials would have been easy to control (Ling 2014).

The first decorated stelae did not show the human body in action, but a significant change affected some of the later rock art. Now the evidence is limited to the Alps, South Scandinavia and possibly Atlantic Spain and Portugal.

Where rock art remained important, the main development was a closer integration between portrayals of weapons or ornaments and depictions of the human body. That is because the swords, spears, helmets and shields were shown in use. There are some of the first explicit depictions of violence since the period of Levantine Art. The rock art of Sweden and Norway is especially informative. During the Early Bronze Age, images of weapons were created near the coast. Some of them were shown singly or in groups, and they were not necessarily connected with drawings of people. There are obvious exceptions – for example, individuals carrying outsize axes or spears – but these weapons could also be shown as exotic artefacts. In later petroglyphs, the weapons were more often associated with human bodies. Something of this contrast is shown by Malmer's (1981) classification of the designs in North European rock art. His chapter on drawings of *'weapons'* defines three main types: axes, daggers or swords, and spears, most of them represented by self-contained images along the east coast. There are fewer in the rock art of the west. Instead that region plays a greater role in his chapter on *'the human figure'*. Five of his categories are particularly relevant here: there are figures wearing swords, those with axes, and other individuals associated with spears, bows or shields.

This development is paralleled much more clearly in other areas. Scenes of combat featured in the Alps, where there was an equally obvious emphasis on masculinity, emphasised by the pursuit of stags, some of them enormous beasts with outsize antlers. Again there is the earliest evidence of people riding horses. Before the pre-Roman Iron Age it was not practised in the north of Italy, and before that time in Scandinavia, the horse seems to have been a sacred animal (Kveiborg 2018).

Although older panels must have told a story (Ranta et al. 2019), there may have been a more explicit interest in narrative. Where some of the Alpine statue menhirs featured friezes of axes, daggers and halberds, now the weapons formed only parts of panels that showed people fighting. If the first depictions were more like a display of trophies, on Iron Age sites they featured in dramatic scenes. As rock art became increasingly figurative there may have been a smaller emphasis on the locations where it was formed, and fewer panels made such obvious use of the natural properties of the stone.

One feature is particularly well documented. Some of the earlier petroglyphs and paintings had been in secluded settings well away from the areas inhabited in daily life. That was no longer true and now there was a closer connection between them and settlement sites. It is seldom clear whether they were contemporary with one another. In South Scandinavia, panels of pecked decoration could even be buried under deposits of burnt stone when houses were built beside them. There is excavated evidence from Himmstalund on the Baltic coast (Nilsson 2012) and Tanum in the west of Sweden (Petersson & Toreld 2015: 85–146). People may have intended to conceal or even destroy the panels. In other cases, the surface of the rock shows evidence of burning. This might have happened while the petroglyphs were in use. Another possibility is that these sites were cremation pyres. In the same way, at Valcamonica, Iron Age settlements were built near, and even over, the remains of earlier images (Rondini & Marretta 2017; Poggiani Keller 2018). Designs illustrating domestic life were made in the vicinity. The situation is still more confusing close to the Spanish/

Portuguese border where hillforts were established in places that were already associated with petroglyphs (Rey Castiñeira & Soto Barreiro 2001). There is no indication that any of these designs were new, but the layout of the later houses and defences may have acknowledged their importance, and in some cases they were respected and preserved. The same may have happened in the Scottish Iron Age when parts of decorated panels were reused (Hingley 1992: 29). The process was not limited to the pre-Roman period. During the first millennium AD, there are runic inscriptions on the rock art sites at Himmelstalund in Sweden and Kårstad in Norway (Nilsson 2012 and 2017; Lødøen and Mandt 2012b: 162–76). A similar inscription at a petroglyph in north-east England refers to the earlier design as 'a relic' (Beckensall 2006: 110)

By the first millennium BC, rock art was more closely integrated into a series of wider developments which included warfare, the earliest hunters on horseback, and the long-distance movement of metalwork. The same period may have seen the development of maritime chiefdoms in parts of Northern Europe. Towards the end of its currency in the Late Bronze Age and Iron Age, there could have been explicit links between different regional styles. For example, there was an increasing emphasis on masculinity and phallic imagery towards the end of the prehistoric sequences in both Scandinavia (Ling 2014) and the Alps (Bevan 2006). Other connections are postulated between the repertoire of Atlantic rock art and Alpine imagery (Santos Estévez 2013; Sansoni 2015). Links are suggested between regions which are even further apart: pictures in the Alps and South Scandinavia (Winter 2008); the drawings of stags and the sun that feature in Galicia and Sweden (Fredell 2010); the depictions of warriors, weapons and vehicles in South Scandinavia, and those on Late Bronze Age stelae in Iberia (Ling & Koch 2018). Connections between these regions are indicated by portable artefacts and metal analysis. It remains to be seen whether they will be supported by more detailed research. At the time of writing, this work is already under way.

Conclusion

European rock art changed its character more than once between the adoption of farming and the Iron Age. Not surprisingly, that sequence illuminates a series of developments which are familiar from other kinds of evidence. It introduces new issues for it reflected some of the basic processes that affected ancient society, although it would be too much to echo Anati's claim for his account of Valcamonica: 'An enquiry into the formation of European civilisation' (Anati 1976). Until now it has been enough to use the contents of the paintings and drawings to *illustrate* the concerns of people in the past. In view of the sheer number and complexity of these images, that may be insufficient. Perhaps the creation and celebration of rock art *helped these developments to achieve their lasting power.* That is why this distinctive medium has so much to offer contemporary archaeology.

Bibliography

Acosta, P. (1968). *La pintura esquématica en España*. Salamanca: Universidad de Salamanca

Alexander, C. (2009). Power in place: the case of superimposition of rock art images at Pià d'Ort, Valcamonica. In G. Nash & D. Gheorgiu (eds.), *The archaeology of people and territory*. Budapest: Archaeolingua, pp. 269–86

Alves, L. B. (2012). The circle, the cross, and the limits of abstraction and figuration in north-western Iberian rock art. In A. Cochrane & A. M. Jones (eds.), *Visualising the Neolithic*. Oxford: Oxbow, pp. 98–214

Alves, L. B., Bradley, R., & Fábregas Valcarce, R. (2013). Tunnel visions: a decorated cave at El Pedroso, Castille, in the light of fieldwork. *Proceedings of the Prehistoric Society* **79**, 198–214

Alves, L. B., & Comendador Rey, B. (2009). Rochas e metais na Pré-historia para além da físico-química. In L. B. Alves & A. Bettencourt (eds.), *Das montes, das pedras e das aguas*. Braga: Universidade do Minho, pp. 37–54

Alves, L. B., & Comendador Rey, B. (2018). Arte esquemático pintado en el noroeste peninsular: una vision integrada transfronteriza. *Gallaecia* **36**, 11–52

Alves, L. B., & Reis, M. (2017). Tattooed landscapes: a reassessment of Atlantic Art distribution, research methods and chronology in the light of a major rock art assemblage at Monte Faro (Valença), Portugal. *Zephyrus* **80**, 49–67

Anati, E. (1968) *Arte rupestre nelle regioni occidental delle Peninsola Ibérica*. Brescia: Archivi di Arti Preistorica

Anati, E. (1976). *Evolution and style in Cammunan rock art: an enquiry into the formation of European civilisation*. Capo di Ponte: Edizioni del Centro

Anati, E. (1994). *Valcamonica rock art: a new history for Europe*. Capo di Ponte: Edizioni del Centro

Anati, E., & Fradkin, A. (2008). Deciphering mythological narratives in the rock art of Valcamonica: the rock of the phallus. In E. Anati (ed.), *Prehistoric art and ideology*. Oxford: British Archaeological Reports, pp. 3–12

Arcà, A. (2000). Agricultural landscapes in the Neolithic and Copper Age engravings of Valcamonica and Mont Bégo. In G. Nash (ed.), *Symbolising place and space*. Oxford: British Archaeological Reports, pp. 29–40

Arcà, A. (2013). L'arte rupestre nell' Età del Rame: il Mont Bégo. In R. de Marinis (ed.), *L'eta del rame. La pianura padana e le Alpi al tempo di Ötzi*. Brescia: Museo Diocesano Brescia, pp. 141–60

Armirotti, A., de Davide, C., & Weeks, D. (2018). Aosta in epoca preistorica e protostorica alla luce delle recenti indagini archeologiche preventive in ambito urbano. *Revista di Scienze Preistoriche* **68**, 109–40

Atkinson, J. (2016). *Ben Lawers: an archaeological landscape in time.* Edinburgh: Scottish Archaeological Internet Reports **62**

Bahn, P. (2010). *Prehistoric rock art: polemics and progress.* Cambridge; Cambridge University Press

Balbín Behrmann, R. de, et al. (eds.) (2009). *Grabados rupestres de la fachada atlántica europea y africana.* Oxford: British Archaeological Reports

Barfield, L. (1986). Chalcolithic burial ritual in Northern Italy: problems of interpretation. *Dialoghi di archeologia* **2**, 241–8

Barfield, L. (2007). *Excavations in the Riparo Valtenesi: Manerba 1976–1994.* Florence: Instituto di Preistoria e Protostoria

Bea, M., & Pajas. J. (2016) Planteamientos interpretativos para el arte levantino a partir del estudio del abrigo del Arquero de los Callejones Cerrados (Albarracín, Teruel). *Zephyrus* **77**, 59–78

Bea, M., & Rojo, J. (2013). También un arte 'macro-levantino'? El arquero de grandes dimensiones de Val de Charco del Agua Amarga (Alcañiz, Teruel). *Trabajos de Prehistoria* **70**, 166–74

Beckensall, S. (2006). *Prehistoric rock art in Northumberland.* Stroud: Tempus

Bednarik, R. (2016). *Myths about rock art.* Oxford: Archaeopress

Bendrey, R. (2012). From wild to domestic horses: a European perspective. *World Archaeology* **44**, 135–57

Bengtsson, L., & Ling, J. (2008). Scandinavia's most finds rich associated rock art sites. *Adoranten* **2008**, 40–50

Bertilsson. U. (2018). New 3D documentation reveals carved Stone Age and Bronze Age axes at Nämforsen, in Ångermanland, Sweden. *Adoranten* **2018**, 72–91

Bettencourt, A., et al. (2017). Where do horses run? a dialogue between signs and matter in the rock carvings of Fornelos (Viana de Castelo, north-west Portugal). In A. Bettencourt et al. (eds.), *Recorded places, experienced places: the Holocene rock art of the Iberian Atlantic northwest.* Oxford: British Archaeological Reports, pp. 167–78

Bettencourt, A., et al. (eds.) (2017). *Recorded places, experienced places: the Holocene rock art of the Iberian Atlantic north-west.* Oxford: British Archaeological Reports

Bevan, L. (2006). *Worshippers and warriors: reconstructing gender and gender relations in the prehistoric rock art of Naquane National Park, Valcamonica, Brescia, Northern Italy.* Oxford: British Archaeological Reports

Bianco Peroni, V. (1994). *I pugnali nell' Italia continentale*. Stuttgart: Franz Steiner

Binder, D., et al. (2017). Modelling the earliest north-western dispersal of Mediterranean Impressed Wares: new dates and Bayesian chronologies. *Documenta Praehistorica* **44**, 54–77

Bradley, R. (1997). *Rock art and the prehistory of Atlantic Europe*. London: Routledge

Bradley, R. (1998). Daggers drawn: depictions of Bronze Age weapons in Atlantic Europe. In C. Chippindale & P. Taçon (eds.), *The archaeology of rock art*. Cambridge: Cambridge University Press, pp. 130–45

Bradley, R. (2009). *Image and audience: rethinking prehistoric art*. Oxford: Oxford University Press

Bradley, R. (2015). Mixed media, mixed messages: religious transmission in Bronze Age Scandinavia. In P. Skoglund, J. Ling & U. Bertilsson (eds.), *Picturing the Bronze Age*. Oxford: Oxbow, 37–45

Bradley, R. (2017). *A geography of offerings: deposits of valuables in the landscapes of ancient Europe*. Oxford: Oxbow

Bradley, R., et al. (2003). Sailing through stone: carved ships and the rock face at Revheim, southwest Norway. *Norwegian Archaeological Review* **35(2)**, 109–18

Bradley, R., & Fábregas Valcarce, R. (1996). Petroglifos gallegos y arte esquemático: una propuesta de trabajo. *Complutum Extra* **6(ii)**, 103–10

Bradley, R., & Watson, A. (2019). Found architecture: interpreting a cup-marked outcrop in the Southern Highlands of Scotland. *Time and Mind* **12**, 3–31

Bradley, R., Watson, A., & Anderson-Whymark, H. (2013). Excavations at four prehistoric rock carvings on the Ben Lawers Estate, Perth and Kinross, 2007–2010. *Proceedings of the Society of Antiquaries of Scotland* **142**, 27–61

Brady, L., Hampson, J., & Sanz, D. (2018). Recording rock art: strategies, challenges and embracing the digital revolution. In B. David & I. McNiven (eds.), *The Oxford handbook of the archaeology and anthropology of rock art*. Oxford: Oxford University Press, pp. 763–85

Breuil, H. (1933–5). *Les peintures schématiques dans la Péninsule Ibérique*, tomes 1–4. Lagny sur Marne: Grévin

Bueno Ramírez, P., & Balbín Behrmann, R. de (2000). Art mégalithique and art en plein air: à propos la definition pour les groupes producteurs dans la Péninsule Ibérique. *L'anthropologie* **104**, 427–58

Bueno Ramírez, P., & Balbín Behrmann, R. de (2016). De cazadores a productores. Transiciones y tradiciones. In *Del neolítico a l'edad del bronze en el Mediterrani occidental. Estudios en homenaje a Bernat Martí Oliver.*

Valencia: Servicio de investigación prehistórica del Museo de Prehistoria de Valencia, pp. 465–80

Bueno Ramírez, P., Balbín Behrmann, R. de, & Barroso Bermejo, L. (2007). Chronologie de l'art mégalithique Iberique. *L'anthropologie* **111**, 590–654.

Bueno Ramírez, P., Balbín Behrmann, R. de, & Barroso Bermejo, L. (2009). Constructadores di megaliticos y marcadores gráficas. Diacronías y sincronías en el Atlántico Ibérico. In R. de Balbín Behrmann (ed.), *Grabados rupestres de la fachada atlántica europea y Africana*. Oxford: British Archaeological Reports, pp. 149–72

Bueno Ramírez, P., Balbín Behrmann, R. de, & Barroso Bermejo, L. (2012). La frontera ideólogica: graficós postglaciares ibéricas. *Trabalhos de Arqueologia* **54**, 139–60

Bueno Ramírez, P., Balbín Behrmann, R. de, & Barroso Bermejo, L. (2013). Símbolos para los muertos, símbolos para los vivos en Andalucía. In J. Martínez García & M. Hernández Pérez (eds.), *Actas del II congreso del arte rupestre esquemático en la Penninsula Ibérica*. Los Vélez: Comarca de Los Vélez, pp. 25–48

Bueno Ramírez, P., Balbín Behrmann, R. de, & Barroso Bermejo, L. (2015). Graphic programmes as ideological construction of the megaliths: the south of the Iberian Peninsula as case study. In L. Rocha, P. Bueno Ramírez & G. Branco (eds.), *Death as archaeology of transition: thoughts and materials*. Oxford: British Archaeological Reports, pp. 51–69

Bueno Ramírez, P., Barroso Bermejo L., & Balbín Behrmann, R. de (2008). *Graphical marks and the megalith builders of the International Tagus, Iberian Peninsula*. Oxford: British Archaeological Reports

Bueno Ramírez, P., et al. (2016). Stones before stones: reused stelae and menhirs in Galician megaliths. In R. Fábregas Valcarce & C. Rodríguez Rellán (eds.), *Public images, private readings: multi-perspective approaches to the post-Palaeolithic rock art*. Oxford: Archaeopress, pp. 11–16

Bueno Ramírez, P. et al. (2019). From pigment to symbol: the role of paintings in the ideological construction of European megaliths. In J. Müller, M. Hinz & M. Wunderlich (eds.), *Megaliths, societies, landscapes. Early monumentality and social differentiation in Neolithic Europe*, vol. 3. Bonn: Rudolf Habelt, pp. 845–64

Burenhult, G. (1973). *The rock carvings of Götland*, part 2. Lund: Acta Archaeologica Lundensia

Capelle, T. (2008). *Bildwelden der Bronzezeit: Fesbilder in Norddeuschland und Skandinavien*. Mainz: von Zabern

Carlin, N. (2017). Getting into the groove: exploring the relationship between Grooved Ware and developed passage tombs in Ireland c. 3000 – 2700 BC. *Proceedings of the Prehistoric Society* **83**, 155–88

Casini, S., de Marinis, R., & Pedrotti, A. (1995). *Statue-stele e massi incisi nell' Europa dell' Età del Rame*. Bergamo: Notizie Archeologiche Bergamensi

Casini, S., & de Marinis, R. (2009). Des pierres et des dieux. L 'art rupestre dans la Valettine et du Valcamonica. *Le Globe* **149**, 61–92

Casini, S., & Fossati, A. (2013). Immagini di dei, guerrieri e donne. Stele, massi incisi e arte rupestre dell' età del rame in Valcamonica e Valtellina. In R. de Marinis (ed.), *L'eta del rame. La pianura padana e le Alpi al tempo di Ötzi*. Brescia: Museo Diocesano Brescia, pp. 161–96

Cassen, S. (2009). *Exercise de stèle*. Paris: Errance

Coles, J. (2000). *Patterns in a rocky land: rock carvings in south-west Uppland, Sweden*. Uppsala: Uppsala University

Coles, J. (2005). *Shadows of a northern past: rock carvings of Bohuslän and Østfold*. Oxford: Oxbow

Collado Giraldo, H. (2006). *Arte rupestre en la Cuenca del Guardiana*. Badajoz: Alconchel-Cheles

Collado Giraldo, H. (2016). A mark along the way: Schematic rock art and communication routes. *Arts* **5(6)**, 1–11

Collado Giraldo, H., et al. (2014). El arte rupestre esquématico del Arroyo Barbón: contextualización arqueólogica y characterización de pigmentos. *Zephyrus* **74**, 15–39

Costas Goberna, J., & Novoa Álvarez, P. (1993). *Los grabados rupestres de Galicia*. La Coruña: Museo Aequeloxico

Cremonisi, R., & Tosatti, A. (eds.) (2017). *L'arte rupestre dell' età dei metalli nella peninsola italiana*. Oxford: Archaeopress

Criado Boado, F., Martínez-Cortizas, A., & García Quintela, M. (eds.) (2013). Petroglifos, paleoambiente y paisaje. Estudios interdisciplinares del arte rupestre de Campo Lameiro (Pontevedra). *Traballos de Arqueoloxía e Patrimonio* **43**

Crumlin-Pedersen, O., & Trakadas, A. (2003). *Hjortspring: a pre-Roman Iron Age warship in context*. Roskilde: Viking Ship Museum

Cruz Berrocal, M. (2005). *Paisaje y arte rupestre. Patrones de localización de la pintura levantina*. Oxford: British archaeological Reports

Cruz Berrocal, M., & Vicent García J. (2007). Rock art as an archaeological and social indicator: the Neolithicisation of the Iberian Peninsula. *Journal of Anthropological Archaeology* **26**, 676–97

David, B., et al. (2001). Why digital enhancement of rock art works: rescaling and saturating colours. *Antiquity* **75**, 781–92

Deacon, J. (2001). A /Xan conundrum: what comes first, the art or the place? In K. Helskog (ed.), *Theoretical perspectives in rock art research*. Oslo: Novus forlag, pp. 242–50

Deakin, P. (2007). Exploring links between cupmarks and cairnfields. In A. Mazel, G. Nash & C. Waddington (eds.), *Art as metaphor: the prehistoric rock art of Britain*. Oxford: Archaeopress, pp. 111–22

Devignes, M. (1997). Les rapports entre peintures et gravures dans l'art mégalithique Ibérique. In J. Helgouac'h, C-T Le Roux & J. Lecornec (eds.) *Art et symboles en mégalithisme Européen*. Revue Archéologique de l'Ouest Supplément 8, pp. 9–22

Di Fraia, T. (2011). Raffigurazioni rupestri e culti millenari in Val di Sangro. In E. Anati (ed.), *Arte e comunicazione nelle società pre-letterate*. Milan: Jaca Book Spa, pp. 172–9

Diaz-Guardamino, M. (2010). *Las estelas decoradas en la prehistoria de la Penísula Ibérica*. Madrd: Universidad Complutense de Madrid

Díaz-Guardamino, M. (2014). Shaping social identities in Bronze Age and Early Iron Age western Iberia: the role of funerary practices, stelae and statue-menhirs. *European Journal of Archaeology* 17, 329–49

Dinis, A. P., & Bettencourt, A. (2011). A arte Atlántica de Crastroeiro (norte de Portugal): contextos e significados. *Gallaecia* 28, 41–7

Dolfini, A. (2011). The function of Chalcolithic metalwork in Italy: an assessment based on use-wear analysis. *Journal of Archaeological Science* 38, 1037–49

Dolfini, A. (2013). The emergence of metallurgy in the Central Mediterranean a new model. *European Journal of Archaeology* 16, 21–62

Dronfield, J. (1996). Entering alternative realities: cognition, art and architecture in Irish passage-tombs. *Cambridge Archaeological Journal* 6, 37–72

Earle, T., et al. (2015). The political economy and metal trade in Bronze Age Europe: understanding regional variability in terms of comparative advantages and articulations. *European Journal of Archaeology* 18, 633–57

Enlander, R. (2016). The rock 'artist': exploring processes of interaction in the rock art of the north of Ireland. In H. Chittock & J. Valdez-Tullett (eds.), *Archaeology with art*. Oxford: Archaeopress, pp. 33–52

Eogan, G. (1990). Irish megalithic tombs and Iberian comparisons and contrasts. In *Probleme der Meglithgräberforschung*. Madrid: Deutsches archäologisches Institut, pp. 113–38

Escoriza Mateu, T. (2008). Patriarchy and ideology in the rock art of the west Iberian Mediterranean Basin. In E. Anati (ed.), *Prehistoric art and ideology*. Oxford: British Archaeological Reports, pp. 53–9

Fábregas Valcarce, R. (2009). A context for the Galician rock art. In R. de Balbín Behrmann et al. (eds.), *Grabados rupestres de la fachada atlántica europea y Africana*. Oxford: British Archaeological Reports, pp. 69–83

Fábregas Valcarce, R., et al. (2007). Un petroglifo de tipo outeiro do corno en Porto do Son (A Coruña). *Gallaecia* **26**, 55–68

Fábregas Valcarce, R., Peña Santos, A. de la, & Rodríguígez Rellán, C. (2011). Río de Angueira 2 (A Coruña). Un conxunto exceptional de escena de monta. *Gallaecia* **30**, 29–51

Fábregas Valcarce, R., & Rodríguez Rellán, C. (2012a). *A arte rupestre no norte do Barbanza*. Santiago de Compostela: Andavira Editora

Fábregas Valcarce, R., & Rodríguez Rellán, C. (2012b). A media luz. Grabados en la Prehistoria Reciente en abrigos galaicos. *Trabajos de Prehistoria* **69**, 80–102

Fábregas Valcarce, R., & Rodríguez Rellán, C. (2015). Walking on the stones of years: some remarks on the north-west Iberian rock art. In P. Skoglund, J. Ling & U. Bertilsson (eds.), *Picturing the Bronze Age*. Oxford: Oxbow, pp. 47–63

Fábregas Valcarce, R., Rodríguez Relláan, C., & Rodríguez Álvarez, E. (2011). Representacións de armas no interior de Galicia (Comarca de Deza, Pontevedra). Unha reflexión sobre a distribución e cronoloxía destes motivos. *Gallaecia* **68**, 49–68

Fábregas Valcarce, R., & Vilaseco Vázquez, X.I. (2016). Building forever or just for the time being? A view from north-western Iberia. In L. Laporte & C. Scarre (eds.), *The megalithic architectures of Europe*. Oxford: Oxbow, pp. 37–54

Fages, A. et al. (2019). Tracking five millennia of horse management with extensive ancient genome time series. *Cell* **177**, 1419–35

Fahlander, F. (2013). Articulating relations: a non-representational view of Scandinavian rock art. In B. Alberti, A. Meirion Jones and J. Pollard (eds.), *Archaeology after interpretation*. Walnut Creek: Left Coast Presss, pp. 305–24

Fahlander, F. (2019). Petroglyphs as 'contraptions' – animacy and vitalist technologies in a Bronze Age archipelago. *Time and Mind* **12**, 109–20

Fairén Jiménez, S. (2006). *El paisaje de la neolitización*. Alicante: Universidad de Alicante

Fairén Jiménez, S. (2007). British Neolithic rock art in its landscape. *Journal of Field Archaeology* **32**, 283–95

Fairén Jiménez, S. (2015). Neolithic rock art in Iberia. In C. Fowler, J. Harding & D. Hofmann (eds.), *The Oxford handbook of Neolithic Europe*. Oxford: Oxford University Press, pp. 839–55

Fedele, F. (2008). Statue-menhirs, human remains and *mana* at the Ossimo 'Anvoia' ceremonial site, Val Camonica. *Journal of Mediterranean Archaeology* **21**, 57–79

Fedele, F. (2013). Il sito ceremoniale di Anvoia (Valcamonica). In R. de Marinis (ed.) 2013. *L'eta del rame. La pianura padana e le Alpi al tempo di Ötzi.* Brescia: Museo Diocesano Brescia, pp. 197–207

Fedele, F. (2015). Life and death of Copper Age monoliths at Ossimo Anvoia (Val Camonica, Central Alps) 3000 BC – AD 1950. In M. Díaz-Guardamino, L. García Sanjuan & D. Wheatley (eds.), *The lives of prehistoric monuments in Iron Age, Roman and Medieval Europe.* Oxford: Oxford University Press, pp. 225–48

Fedele, J., & Fossati, A. (2012). L'area ceremoniale di Anvoia a Ossimo, Valcamonica: i monoliti simbolici e il loro contesto. *Preistoria Alpina* **46**.2, 187–99

Fernández López de Pablo, J. (2006). Las flechas en el arte Levantino. *Archivo de Prehistoria Levantina* **26**, 101–59

Fernández López de Pablo, J. (2014). Traditions artistiques, interactions culturelles et contextes symboliques de la transition Néolithique dans la région Méditerranéen espagnol. In C. Manem, J. Perrin & J. Guilaine (eds.), *Le transition Néolithique en Mediterranée.* Arles: Errance, pp. 371–403

Fernández Quintano, J. (2013). Consideraciones sobre los motivos astraliformes en el arte en la Península Ibérica. In J. Martínez García & M. Hernández Pérez (eds.), *Actas del II congreso de arte rupestre esquemático en la Peninsula Ibérica.* Los Vélez: Comarca de Los Vélez, pp. 10–24

Forsberg, L. (2006). Tidig hällkonst och koloniseringen av taigaområdet i Mittnorde. In R. Barndon et al. (eds.), *Samfunn, symboler og identitet.* Bergen: Universitet i Bergen, pp. 87–103

Fossati, A. (2002). Landscape representations on boulders and menhirs in the Valcamonica – Valtellina area, Alpine Italy. In G. Nash & C. Chippindale (eds.), *European landscapes of rock art.* London: Routledge, pp. 93–115

Fossati, A. (2015). The rock art traditions of Valcamonica – Valtellina during the Neolithic period. In C. Fowler, J. Harding & D. Hofmann (eds.), *The Oxford handbook of Neolithic Europe.* Oxford: Oxford University Press, pp. 857–870

Fredell, Å (2010). A mo(ve)ent in time: a comparative study of a rock-art picture in Galicia and Bohuslän. In Å. Fredell, K. Kristiansen & F. Criado Boado (eds.), *Representations and communications: creating an archaeological matrix of late prehistoric art.* Oxford: Oxbow, pp. 52–74

Frodsham, P. (1996). Spirals in time: Morwick Mill and the spiral motif in the British Neolithic. *Northern Archaeology* **13/14**, 101–38

Fuglesvedt, I. (2017). *Rock art and the wild mind: visual imagery in Mesolithic Northern Europe.* Abingdon: Routledge

Gallay, A. (2011). *Autour de Petit-Chasseur.* Paris: Errance

Garcês, S., and Oosterbeek, L. (2020).The Tagus Valley rock art. In C. Scarre and L. Oosterbeek (eds.), *Megalithic tombs in western Iberia: excavations at the Anta da Lajinha.* Oxford: Oxbow, pp.171–88

García Arranz, J., Collado Giraldo, H., & Nash, G. (eds.) (2012). *The Levantine question: post-Palaeolithic rock art in the Iberian Peninsula.* Cáceres: Universidad de Extremadura

García de Lagrán, I., Fernández Domínguez, E. & Rojo Guerra, M. (2018). Solutions or illusions? An analysis of the available palaeogenetic evidence from the origins of the Neolithic in the Iberian Peninsula. *Quaternary International* **470**, 353–68

García Quintela, M., & Santos Estévez, M. (2015). Astronomical significance in Bronze Age and Iron Age rock art. In C. Ruggles (ed.), *Handbook of archaeoastronomy and ethnoastronomy.* New York: Springer, pp. 1214–1222

García Sanjuán, L. (1999). Expressions of inequality: settlement patterns, economy and social organisation in the south-west Iberian Bronze Age (c. 1700 – 1100 BC). *Antiquity* **73**, 337–51,

Gjerde, J. M. (2010). *Rock art and landscapes: studies of Stone Age rock art from northern Fennoscandia.* Trømsø: University of Trømsø

Gjerde, J. M. (2012). Stone Age rock art and beluga landscapes at River Vyg, north-western Russsia. *Fennoscandia Archaeologica* **30**, 37–54

Gjerde, J. M. (2017). A boat journey in rock art from the Bronze Age to the Stone Age: from the Stone Age to the Bronze Age in northernmost Europe. In P. Skoglund, J. Ling & U. Bertilssson (eds.), *North meets south: theoretical aspects on the northern and southern rock art traditions in Scandinavia.* Oxford: Oxbow, pp. 113–43

Gjessing, G. (1935). Die Chronologie der Schiffdarstellung auf den Felsenzeichnungen zu Bardal, Trøndelag. *Acta Archaeologica* **6**, 125–39

Gjessing, G. (1936). *Nordenfjelske ristninger og malinger av den arktiske gruppe.* Oslo: Instituttet for Sammenlijnende Kulturfoskning

Glob, P. (1969). *Helleristninger I Danmark.* Copenhagen: Nordisk forlag

Goldhahn, J. (2002). Roaring rocks: an audio-visual perspective on hunter-gatherer engravings in northern Sweden and Scandinavia. *Norwegian Archaeological Review* **35**, 29–61

Goldhahn, J. (2010). Emplacement and the *hau* of rock art. In J. Goldhahn, I. Fugelstvedt & A. Jones (eds.) *Changing pictures: rock art traditions and visions in Northern Europe.* Oxford: Oxbow, pp. 106–26

Goldhahn, J. (2013). *Bredarör på Kivik: en arkeologisk odyssé*. Kalmar: Kalmar Studies in Archaeology

Goldhahn, J. (2014). Engraved biographies: rock art and the life-histories of Bronze Age objects. *Current Swedish Archaeology* **22**, 97–136

Goldhahn, J. (2016). *Sagaholm: North European rock art and burial ritual*. Oxford: Archaeopress

Goldhahn, J. (2018). North European rock art: a long-term perspective. In B. David & I. McNiven (eds.), *The Oxford handbook of the archaeology and anthropology of rock art*. Oxford: Oxford University Press, pp. 51–72

Goldhahn, J. (2019a). On unfolding present and past (rock art) worldlings. *Time and Mind* **12**, 63–77

Goldhahn, J. (2019b). *Birds in the Bronze Age: a North European perspective*. Cambridge: Cambridge University Press

Goldhahn, J., & Ling, J. (2013). Bronze Age rock art in Northern Europe: contexts and interpretations. In H. Fokkens & A. Harding (eds.), *The Oxford handbook of the European Bonze Age*. Oxford: Oxford University Press, pp. 270–90

Goldhahn, J., & May, S. eds. (2019). Beyond the global encounter: approaching contact rock art studies. *Australian Archaeology* **85**

Gomes, M. V. (1983). Arte esquemática do Vale do Tejo. *Zephyrus* **36**, 279–89

Hameau, P. (2002). *Passage, transformation et art schématique: l'exemple des peintures Néolithiques du sud de la France*. Oxford: British Archaeological Reports

Hameau, P. (2003). Aspects de l'art rupestre en France Mediterranéen. In J. Guilaine (ed.), *Arts et symboles du Néolithique à la Protohistoire*. Paris: Errance, pp. 137–63

Hameau, P. (2005). Des goûts des couleurs: Chronologie relative et identité culturelle à travers l'analyse des peintures schématiques du Néolithique dans le sud de la France. *Zephyrus* **58**, 95–211

Hameau, P. (2007). Cloistering and gathering places and Neolithic graphic expression. *L'anthropologie* **111**, 721–51

Hameau, P., & Painaud, A. (2009). Ritos de paso y abrigos pintados en el Neolítico. *Zephyrus* **63**, 61–70

Hameau, P., & Painaud, A. (2011). Le géste et la forme dans l'expression graffique du Néolithique. *Zephyrus* **67**, 91–110

Harris, S. (2003). Representations of woven textiles in Alpine Europe during the Copper Age. In J. Wilkin & E. Herring (eds.), *Inhabiting symbols: symbol and image in the ancient Mediterranean*. London: Acccordia Research Institute, pp. 43–84

Harrison, R. (2004). *Symbols and warriors. Images of the European Bronze Age.* Bristol: Western Academic Press

Harrison, R., & Heyd, V. (2007). The transformation of Europe in the third millennium BC: the example of 'Le Petit Chasseur I + III (Sion, Valais, Switzerland). *Praehistorische Zeitschrift* **82**, 129–214

Hauptmann Wahlgren, K. (2002). *Bilder av betydelse.* Lindome: Bricoleur Press

Helskog, K. (1999). The shore connection: cognitive landscape and communication with rock carvings in northernmost Europe. *Norwegian Archaeological Review* **32**, 73–94

Helskog, K. (2012). Bears and meanings among the hunter-fisher-gatherers in North Fennoscandia 9000 – 2500 BC. *Cambridge Archaeological Journal* **22**, 209–36

Helskog, K. (2014). *Communicating with a world of beings: the World Heritage rock art sites at Alta, Arctic Norway.* Oxford: Oxbow

Hernández Pérez, M (2006). Artes esquemáticos en el Peninsula Ibérica: el paradigma de la pintura esquemática. In J. Martínez García & M. Hernández Pérez (eds.), *Arte rupestre esquemático en la Peninsula Ibérica.* Los Vélez: Comarca de Los Vélez, pp. 13–31

Herva, V.-P., & Lahelma, A. (2019). *Northern archaeology and cosmology: a relational view.* Abingdon: Routledge

Herva V.-P., & Ylimaunu, T. (2014). Coastal cosmologies: long-term perspectives on the perception and understanding of dynamic coastal landscapes in the Northern Baltic Sea region. *Time and Mind* **7**, 183–202

Hingley, R. (1992). Society in Scotland from 700 BC to AD 200. *Proceedings of the Society of Antiquaries of Scotland* **122**, 7–53

Horn, C. (2018). Fast like a war canoe: pragmamorphism in Scandinavian rock art. In A. Dolfini et al. (eds.), *Prehistoric warfare and violence: quantitative and qualitative approaches.* New York: Springer, pp. 109–27

Horn, C., et al. (2018). By all means necessary: 2.5D and 3D recording of surfaces in the study of South Scandinavian rock art. *Open Archaeology* **4**, 81–96

Horn, C., Potter, R., & Pitman, D. (2019). An evaluation of the visualisation and interpretive potential of applying GIS data processing techniques to 3D rock art data. *Journal of Archaeological Science Sciences Reports* **27**, 101971

Huet, T. (2017). New perspectives on the chronology and meaning of Mont Bego rock art (Alpes-Maritimes, France). *Cambridge Archaeological Journal* **27**, 199–221

Huet, T. (2018). *Les gravures piquetées du Mont Bego (Alpes-Maritimes): Organisation spatiale et sériation.* Paris: Société Préhistorique Française

Huet, T., & Bianchi, N. (2016). A study of the Roche de l'Autel's pecked engravings, Les Merveilles sector, Mont Bego area (Alpes-Maritimes, France). *Journal of Archaeological Science Science Reports* **5**, 105–18

Hurtado Pérez, V. (2008). *Ídolos, estilos y territorio de los primeros campesinos en el sur peninsular: Acercándonos al pasado, prehistoria en 4 actas*. Madrid: Ministero de Cultura, pp. 1–11

Jiménez Jáimez, V. (2015). The unsuspected circles: on the late recognition of Iberian Neolithic and Chalcolithic enclosures. *Proceedings of the Prehistoric Society* **81**, 179–98

Jones, A., & Kirkham, G. (2013). From landscape to portable art: the changing settings of simple rock art in south-western Britain and its wider context. *European Journal of Archaeology* **16**, 636–59

Jones, A. M. (2017). Rock art and ontology. *Annual Review of Anthropology* **46**, 167–81

Jones, A. M., & Cochrane, A. (2018). *The archaeology of art: methods, practices, affects*. Abingdon: Routledge

Jones, A. M., & Díaz-Guardamino, M. (2019). *Making a mark: image and process in Neolithic Britain and Ireland*. Oxford: Oxbow

Jones, A. M., et al. (2011). *An animate landscape: rock art and the prehistory of Kilmartin, Argyll, Scotland*. Oxford: Windgather Press

Jorge, S. (ed.) (2003). *Recintos murados da Pré-Historia recente*. Porto: Uninversidade do Porto

Kaul, F. (1998). *Ships on bronzes. A study in Bronze Age religion and iconography*. Copenhagen: National Museum

Kaul, F. (2014). The northernmost rock carvings belonging to the Bronze Age tradition. In H. C. Gullow (ed.), *Northern worlds: landscapes, interactions and dynamics*. Copenhagen: National Museum, pp. 115–28

Kaul, F. (2017). Bronze Age archaeology and cosmology: dialogues at the crossroads. *Acta Archaeologica* **88**, 35–56

Keates, S. (2000). The ancestralization of the landscape: monumentality and the rock art of the Copper Age Valcamonica. In G. Nash (ed.), *Symbolising place and space*. Oxford: British Archaeological Reports, pp. 83–102

Kristiansen, K. (2012). Rock art and religion. The sun journey in Indo-European mythology and Bronze Age rock art. *Adoranten* **2012**, 69–86

Kristiansen, K., & Larsson, T. (2005). *The rise of Bronze Age society: travels, transmissions and transformations*. Cambridge: Cambridge University Press

Kunst, M. (2017). Zambujal 2013. Ein kuperzeitliche befistigte Gross-Siedlung? *Madrider Mitteilungen* **58**, 1–30

Kveiborg, J. (2018). Traversing earth and sky: the Nordic Bronze Age horse in a long-term perspective. *Praehistorische Zeitschrift* **93**, 225–64

Lahelma, A. (2008). *A touch of red: archaeological and ethnographic approaches to interpreting Finnish rock paintings.* Helsinki: Finnish Antiquarian Society

Lahelma, A. (2017). The circumpolar context of the 'sun ship' motif in South Scandinavian rock art. In P. Skoglund, J. Ling & U. Bertilssson (eds.), *North meets south: Theoretical aspects on the northern and southern rock art traditions in Scandinavia.* Oxford: Oxbow, pp. 144–71

Lewis-Williams, D., & Dowson, T. (1988). The signs of all times: entoptic phenomena in Upper Palaeolithic art. *Current Anthropology* **29**, 201–45

Lillios, K. (2004). Lives of stone, lives of people: re-viewing the engraved plaques of Late Neolithic and Copper Age Iberia. *European Journal of Archaeology* **7**, 125–58

Lillios, K. (2008). *Heraldry for the dead.* Austin: University of Texas Press

Lillios, K. (2020). *The archaeology of the Iberian Peninsula: from the Palaeolithic to the Bronze Age.* Cambridge: Cambridge University Press

Ling, J. (2013). *Rock art and seascapes in Uppland.* Oxford: Oxbow

Ling, J. (2014). *Elevated rock art: towards a maritime understanding of Bronze Age rock art in northern Bohuslän, Sweden.* Oxford: Oxbow

Ling, J., & Cornell, P. (2017). Violence, warriors and rock art in Bronze Age Scandinavia. In R. Chacon & R. Mendoza (eds.), *Feast, famine or fighting? Multiple pathways to social complexity.* New York: Springer, pp. 15–33

Ling, J., Earle, T., & Kristiansen, K. (2018). Maritime mode of production: raiding and trading in seafaring chiefdoms. *Current Anthropology* **59**, 488–524

Ling, J., et al. (2013). Moving metals or indigenous mining? Provenancing Scandinavian Bronze Age metalwork by lead isotopes and trace elements. *Journal of Archaeological Science* **40**, 291–304

Ling, J., & Koch, J. (2018). A sea beyond Europe to the north and west. In J. Dodd and E. Meizer (eds.), *Giving the past a future.* Oxford: Archaeopress, pp. 96–111

Ling, J., & Uhnér, C. (2014). Rock art and metal trade. *Adoranten* **2014**, 23–43

Lødøen, T. (2010). Concepts of rock in Late Mesolithic western Norway. In J. Goldhahn, I. Fuglesvedt and A. Jones (eds.), *Changing pictures: rock art traditions and visions in northernmost Europe.* Oxford: Oxbow, pp. 35–47

Lødøen, T. (2015). The method and physical process behind the making of hunters' art in Western Norway: the experimental production of images. In H. Stebergløkken et al. (eds.), *Ritual landscapes and borders within rock art research.* Oxford: Archaeopress, pp.67–77

Lødøen, T., & Mandt, G. (2012a). *Vingen. Et naturens kolossalmuseum for helleristninger.* Trondheim: Akademika forlag

Lødøen, T., & Mandt, G. (2012b). *The rock art of Norway*. Oxford: Oxbow

López-Montalvo, E. (2015). Violence in Neolithic Iberia: new readings of Levantine art. *Antiquity* **89**, 309–25

López-Montalvo, E. (2018). Hunting scenes in Spanish Levantine art: an unequivocal chrono-cultural marker of Epipalaeolithic and Mesolithic Iberian societies? *Quaternary International* **472**, 205–20

López-Montalvo, E., et al. (2014). An approximation to the study of black pigments in Cova Remigia (Castellón, Spain): technical and cultural assessments of the use of carbon-based black pigments in Spanish Levantine rock art. *Journal of Archaeological Science* **52**, 535–45

de Lumley, H. (1995). *Le grandiose et le sacré*. Aix-en-Provence: Édisud

de Lumley, H., & Echassoux, A. (2009). Les gravures rupestres de Chalcolithique et du l'âge du Bronze ancient du Mont Bego. Les mythes cosmogoniques des premiers peoples metallurgistes des Alpes méridionales. *L'Anthropologie* **113**, 969–1004

MacWhite, E. (1946). A new view of the Irish Bronze Age rock-scribings. *Journal of the Royal Society of Antiquaries of Ireland* **76**, 59–80

Malmer, M. (1981). *A chorological study of North European rock art*. Stockholm: Almqvist and Wiksell

Manem, C. (2014). Dynamiques spatio-temporelles et culturelles de la Néolithicisation Ouest-Mediterranée. In C. Manem, J. Perrin & J. Guilaine (eds.), *Le transition Néolithique en Mediterranée*. Arles: Errance, pp. 419–38

de Marinis, R. (2013). La necropoli di Remedello Sotto e l'età del Rame nella pianura a nord del Po. In R. de Marinis (ed.) 2013. *L'eta del rame. La pianura padana e le Alpi al tempo di Ötzi*. Brescia: Museo Diocesano Brescia, pp. 301–51

de Marinis, R. (ed.) (2013). *L'eta del rame. La pianura padana e le Alpi al tempo di Ötzi*. Brescia: Museo Diocesano di Brescia

de Marinis, R., Dalmeri, G., & Pedrotti, A. (eds.) (2012). *L'arte preistorica in Italia*. Trento: Istituto Italiano di preistoria e protostoria

de Marinis, R., & Fossati, A. (2012). A che punto è lo studio dell' arte rupestre della Valcamonica. *Preistoria Alpina* **46.2**, 17–43

de Marinis, R., & Valzolgher, E. (2013). Riti funerari dell' antica età bel Bronzo in area padana. In R. de Marinis (ed.), *L'eta del rame. La pianura padana e le Alpi al tempo di Ötzi*. Brescia: Museo Diocesano Brescia, pp. 545–5

Marretta, A. (2013). Age of the heroes: a brief overview of Valcamonica rock art during the Iron Age. *Adoranten* **2013**, 1–14.

Marretta, A. (2014). Where it all began: the Copper Age roots of Valcamonica. *Adoranten* **2014**, 52–67

Marretta, A. (2018). *La roccia 12 del Seradina 1*. Capo da Ponte: Edizione del Parco Seradina-Bedolina

Martí Oliver, B., & Bernabeu Aubán, J. (2014). Les premiers groups agropastorales de la péninsule Ibérique. In C. Manem, J. Perrin & J. Guilaine (eds.), *Le transition Néolithique en Mediterranée*. Arles: Errance, pp. 419–38

Martín Socas, D., & Camalich Massieu, M. (1982). La 'Cerámica Simbólica' y su problemática. *Cuadernos de Prehistoria de la Universidad de Granada* **7**, 267–306

Martín Valls, R. (1983). Las insculturas del castro salmantino de Yecla de Yeltes y sus relaciones con los petroglifos gallegos. *Zephyrus* **36**, 217–31

Martínez García, J., & Hernández Pérez, M. (eds.) (2000). *Arte rupestre esquemático en la Penninsula Ibérica*. Los Vélez: Comarca de Los Vélez

Martínez i Rubio, T., & Martorell Rubio, X. (2012). La senda heredada: contribución al estudio de la red de caminos óptimos entre yacimientos de hábitat y el arte rupestre neolíticos en el macizo del Caroig (Valencia). *Zephyrus* **70**, 69–84

Matteoli, T. (2012). L'arte rupestre preistorica e protistorica in Umbria. *Preistoria Alpina* **46(2)**, 99–107

Matteoli, T., et al. (2017). Echoing landscapes: echolocation and the placement of rock art in the Central Mediterranean. *Journal of Archaeological Science* **83**, 12–25.

Maura Mijares, R. (2010). *Piñas de Cabrera*. Sevilla: Junta de Andalucía

Melheim, L., & Ling, J. (2017). Taking the stranger on board: two maritime legacies of Bronze Age rock art. In P. Skoglund, J. Ling & U. Bertilsson (eds.), *North meets south: theoretical aspects on the northern and southern rock art traditions in Scandinavia*. Oxford: Oxbow, pp. 59–86

Mezzena, F. (1998). Les stèles anthropomophes de l'aire mégalithique d'Aoste In A. M. Belley et al. (eds.), *Dei di pietra*. Skira: Regione autonoma Valle d'Aosta, pp. 90–121

Milstreu, G. (2017). Recut rock art images (with a special emphasis on ship carvings). In S. Bergerbrant & A. Wessman (eds.), *New perspectives on the Bronze Age*. Oxford: Archaeopress, pp. 281–7

Moro Abadía, O., and González Morale, M. (in press). Art in the making: recent developments in the study of Pleistocene and Holocene images. *Journal of Archaeological Method and Theory*

Needham, S. (2015). A hafted halberd excavated at Trecastell, Powys: from undercurrent to uptake – the emergence and contextualisation of halberds in Wales and north-west Europe. *Proceedings of the Prehistoric Society* **81**, 1–41

Nielsen, S., Persson, P., & Solheim, S. (2019). De-Neolithicisation in southern Norway inferred from statistical modelling of radiocarbon dates. *Journal of Anthropological Archaeology* **53**, 82–91

Nilsson, P. (2012). Reused rock art: traces of Iron Age activities at Bronze Age rock art sites. In R. Berge, M. Jasinski & K. Sognnes (eds.), *N-TAG TEN*. Oxford: Archaeopress, pp. 19–30

Nilsson, P. (2017). *Brukade bilder*. Stockholm: Institute for Archaeology and Classical Culture

Nimura, C. (2016). *Prehistoric rock art in Scandinavia: agency and environmental change*. Oxford: Oxbow

Nimura, C., Skoglund, P., & Bradley, R. (2020). Navigating inland: Bronze Age watercraft and the lakes of southern Sweden. *European Journal of Archaeology* **23**, 186–206

Nord, J. (2009). *Changing landscapes and persistent places: an exploration of the Bjäre Peninsula*. Lund: Lund University Department of Archaeology and Ancient History

Nordenborg Myhre, L. (2004). *Trialectic archaeology: monuments and space in southwest Norway*. Stavanger: Museum i Stavanger

O'Brien, W. (2012). *Iverni: a prehistory of Cork*. Cork: The Collins Press

O'Brien, W. (2015). *Prehistoric copper mining in Europe 5500 – 500 BC*. Oxford: Oxford University Press

O'Connor, B. (2006). *Inscribed landscapes: contextualising prehistoric rock art in Ireland*. Doctoral thesis, University College, Dublin

O'Sullivan, M. (1997). Megalithic art in Ireland and Brittany. Divergence or convergence? In J. L'Helgouac'h, C.-T. Le Roux & J. Lecornec (eds.) *Art et symboles en mégalithisme Européen*. Revue Archéologique de l'Ouest Supplément 8, pp. 81–96

Olalde, I., et al. (2019). The genomic history of the Iberian Peninsula over the last 8000 years. *Science* **363**, 1230–4.

Oosterbeck, L. (2009). Water and symbols in western Iberian late prehistory. In F. Djíndjian & L. Oosterbeck (eds.), *Symbolic spaces in prehistoric art*. Oxford: British Archaeological Reports, pp. 105–11

Pailler, Y., & Nicolas, C. (2016). Des dalles ornées durant le Campaniforme et l'Âge du Bronze ancien en Bretagne: mythe ou realité? *Bulletin de la Société Préhistorique Française* **113**, 333–69

Pariboni, E., et al. (2012). Lo scavo delle statue-stele di Groppoli ed altre ricerche nel territorio di Mulazzo. *Preistoria Alpina* **46.2**, 235–44

Peña Santos, A. de la (1981). Comentario a 'La Pedra das Ferreduras' de Cesare Giulio Borgna. *El Museo de Pontevedra* **35**, 3–8

Peruchetti, L., et al. (2017). Physical barriers, cultural connections: prehistoric metallurgy across the Alpine region. *European Journal of Archaeology* **18**, 599–632

Petersson, H.,& Toreld, C. (eds.) (2015). *Domestic life in the Tanum rock carving area*. Uddevalla: Bohusläns Museum forlag

Pétrequin, P., et al. (eds.) (2012). *Grands haches alpines du Néolithique, Ve et IVe millénaires avant J-C*, tomes 1 and 2. Besançon: Presses Universitaires de Franche-Comté.

Pétrequin, P., Pétrequin, A.-M. & Gauthier, E. (eds.) (2017). *Jade 3–4. Objets-signes et l'interprétation sociales des jades alpins dans l'Europe néolithique.* Besançon: Presses Universitaires de Franche-Comté.

Poggiani Keller, R. (2018). Copper Age ancestral sanctuaries and landscapes in Valle Camonica. In E. Herring & E. O'Donaghue (eds.), *Papers in Italian Archaeology* 7. Oxford: Archaeopress, pp. 431–42

Prendergast, F., et al. (2017). Facing the sun. *Archaeology Ireland* **31(4)**, 10–17

Quintas González, F., & Espejo Guardiola, T. (2008). O Monte das Ferraduras (Fentáns, Cotobade) novos archádegos de arte rupestre. *Estudios Gallegos* **55**, 53–72

Randsborg, K. (1980). *The Viking Age in Denmark*. London: Duckworth

Rainio, R., et al. (2018). Acoustic measurements and digital images processing suggest a link between sound rituals and sacred sites in northern Finland. *Journal of Archaeological Method and Theory* **25**, 453–74

Ranta, M., et al. (2019) Levels of narrativity in Scandinavian Bronze Age petroglyphs. *Cambridge Archaeological Journal* **29**, 497–516

Rey Castiñeira, J., & Soto Barreiro, M .J. (2001). El arte rupestre de Crastoeiro y la problemática de los petroglifos en castros. In A. Dinis, *O povado da Idade do Ferro do Crastroeiro (Mondin de Basto), norte de Portugal*. Braga: Universidade do Minho, pp. 159–200

Robb, J. (2009). People of stone: stelae, personhood and society in prehistoric Europe. *Journal of Archaeological Method and Theory* **16**, 162–83

Robb, J. (2015). Prehistoric art in Europe: a deep-time social history. *American Antiquity* **80**, 635–54

Robb, J. (in press). Continental scale in visual culture: the development of narrative art in prehistoric Europe. *Journal of Archaeological Method and Theory*

Robin, G. (2009). *L'architecture des signes*. Rennes: Presses Universitaires de Rennes

Robin, G. (ed.) (2015) Digital imaging techniques for the study of prehistoric rock art. *Digital Applications in Archaeology and Cultural Heritage* **2**

Rodríguez-Corral, J. (2019). Arming landscape: connectivity and resistance in northwestern Iberia in late prehistory. *Journal of Anthropological Archaeology* **53**, 288–30

Rodríguez Rellán, C., & Fábregas Valcarce, R. (2016). Measuring the spatially-related perceptibility of prehistoric art: some preliminary notes. In R. Fábregas Valcarce & C. Rodriguígez Rellán (eds.), *Public images, private readings: multi-perspective approaches to the Post-Palaeolithic rock art.* Oxford: Archaeopress, pp. 41–50

Rodríguez Rellán, C., Fábregas Valcarce, R., & Carrera Ramírez, F. (in press). Intervención arqueológica en el abrigo Cova dos Mouros (Baleira, Lugo). Un primer ejemplo de pintura esquemática en Galicia. *Munibe* **70**

Rodríguez Rellán, C., Gorgosa López, R., & Fábregas Valcarce, R. (2008). O conxunto dos petroglifos de Campo da Uz e as vías de tránsito cara o interior lucense. *Gallaecia* **27**, 35–61.

Rodríguez Rellán, C, Vázquez Martínez, A., & Fábregas Valcarce, R. (2018). Cifras e imágenes: una aproximación cuantitativa a los petroglifos gallegos. *Trabajos de Prehistoria* **75**, 109–27

Rogerio-Candelera, M., et al. (2018). Landmarks of the past in the Antequera megalithic landscape: a multi-disciplinary approach to the Matacabras rock shelter. *Journal of Archaeological Science* **95**, 76–93

Roldán, C., et al. (2018). Proteomic and metagenomic insights into prehistoric Spanish Levantine rock art. *Nature Scientific Reports* **8.1**, 10011

Rondini, P.,& Marretta, A. (2017). Bridging the gap: rock art and archaeological context in the 'Quattro Dossi' area (Capo di Ponte), Valcamonica, Italy. *Adoranten* **2017**, 5–23

Ruiz, J., et al. (2012). Calcium oxalate AMS C 14 dating and chronology of post-Palaeolithic painting in the Iberian Peninsula. Two dates from Abrigo de los Oculados (Henarejos, Cuenca, Spain). *Journal of Archaeological Science* **39**, 2655–2667

Sanches, M. de J., et al. (1998). Land marks: a new approach to the rock art of Trás-os-Montes, northern Portugal. *Journal of Iberian Archaeology* (1998), 85–104

Sanches, M. de J., & Morais, J. (2011). Escarpas rochosas e pinturas na Serra de Passos / St Comba (nordeste de Portugal). *Estudios Pré-historicos* **18**, 71–117

Sansoni, U. (2012). Lo stato della ricerca sul contesto rupestre della Valcamonica: sintesi sulle scoperte, gli studi tematici ed i caratteri di zona. *Preistoria Alpina* **46.2**, 45–54

Sansoni, U. (2015). Alpine and Scandinavian rock art in the Bronze Age: a common cultural matrix in a web of continental influences. In P. Skoglund,

J. Ling & U. Bertilsson (eds.), *Picturing the Bronze Age*. Oxford: Oxbow, pp. 129–41

Santos da Rosa, N. (2018). La tecnología del arte rupestre Levantino. *Cuadernos de Arte Prehistórico* 7, 120–46

Santos Estévez, M. (2013). Atlantic rock art: transformation and tradition during late prehistory. In M. Cruz Berrocal, L. García Sanjuan & A. Gilman (eds.), *The prehistory of Iberia*. Abingdon: Routledge, pp. 331–48

Santos Estévez, M., & Criado Boado, F. (2000). Deconstructing rock art spatial grammar in the Galician Bronze Age. In G. Nash (ed.), *Symbolising place and space*. Oxford: British Archaeological Reports, pp. 111–22

Santos Estévez, M., & Güimil Fariña, A. (2015). The maritime factor in the distribution of Bronze Age rock art in Galicia. In P. Skoglund, J. Ling & U. Bertilsson (eds.), *Picturing the Bronze Age*. Oxford: Oxbow, pp. 143–54

Santos Estévez, M., & Seoane Veiga, Y. (2010). Rock art and archaeological excavation at Campo Lameiro, Galicia. In Å Fredell, K. Kristiansen, & F. Criado Boado, F. (eds.), 2010. *Representations and communications: creating an archaeological matrix of late prehistoric art*. Oxford: Oxbow, pp. 16–30

Saska, A., Bel'skiy, A., & Mizin, V. (2017). New finds of cup marks near the village of Ol'khova. *Fennoscandia Archeologica* 34, 139–45

de Saulieu, G. (2004). *Art rupestre et statues-menhirs dans les Alpes: des pierres et des pouvoirs 3000 – 2000 av. J.-C.* Paris: Errance

de Saulieu, G. (2013). Rock carvings and Alpine statue-menhirs from the Chalcolithic to the Middle Bronze Age. In H. Fokkens & A. Harding (eds.), *The Oxford handbook of the European Bronze Age*. Oxford: Oxford University Press, pp. 291–310

Scarre, C. (2011). *Landscapes of Neolithic Brittany*. Oxford: Oxford University Press

Scarre, C. (2017). Figurines of Western Europe. In T. Insoll (ed.), *The Oxford handbook of prehistoric figurines*. Oxford: Oxford University Press, pp. 877–900

Schulz Paulsson, B. (2017). *Time and stone: the emergence and development of megaliths and megalithic societies in Europe*. Oxford: Archaeopress

Schultz Paulsson, B., Isendahl, C., & Frykman Markurth, F. (2019). Elk heads at sea: maritime hunters and long-distance boat journeys in Stone Age Fennoscandia. *Oxford Journal of Archaeology* 38, 398–419

Seoane Veiga, Y., Prieto Martínez, P., & Dal Zovo, C. (2013). Bell Beaker findings in rock art contexts. In P. Prieto Martínez, and L. Salanova (eds.), *Current research on Bell Beakers*. Santiago de Compostela: ArchaeoPots, pp. 31–9

Sharpe, K. (2012). Reading between the grooves: regional variations in the style and deployment of 'cup and ring' marked stones in Britain and Ireland. In A. Cochrane & A. M. Jones (eds.), *Visualising the Neolithic*. Oxford: Oxbow, pp. 47–63

Shee Twohig, E., et al. (2010). Open-air rock art at Loughcrew, Co. Meath. *Journal of Irish Archaeology* **19**, 1–28

Shennan, S. (2018). *The first farmers of Europe: an evolutionary perspective*. Cambridge: Cambridge University Press

Simpson, J. (1867). *Archaic sculpturings of cups, circles upon stones and rocks in Scotland, England and other countries*. Edinburgh: Edmondston and Douglas

Skoglund, P. (2006). *Hälleristingar i Kronobergs Län*. Lund: University of Lund Institute of Archaeology

Skoglund, P. (2016). *Rock art through time: Scanian rock carvings in the Bronze Age and earliest Iron Age*. Oxford: Oxbow

Skoglund, P., Ling, J., & Bertilssson, U. (eds.) (2017). *North meets south: theoretical aspects on the northern and southern traditions in Scandinavia*. Oxford: Oxbow

Skoglund, P., Nimura, C., & Bradley, R. (2017). Interpretations of footprints in the Bronze Age rock art of South Scandinavia. *Proceedings of the Prehistoric Society* **83**, 289–303

Sobrino Buhigas, R. (1935). *Corpus petroglyphorum Gallaeciae*. Santiago de Compostela: Seminario de Estudios Gallegos

Sognnes, K. (2001). *Prehistoric imagery and landscapes: rock art in Stjørdal, Trondelag, Norway*. Oxford: British Archaeological Reports

Sognnes, K. (2008). Stability and change in Scandinavian rock art: the case of Bardal, Norway. *Acta Archaeologica* **79**, 230–45

Sognnes, K. (2017). *The northern rock art tradition in central Norway*. Oxford: British Archaeological Reports

Thomas, A. (2016). *Art and architecture in Neolithic Orkney*. Oxford: Archaeopress

Tilley, C. (1991). *Material culture and text: the art of ambiguity*. London: Routledge

Tilley, C. (2004). *The materiality of stone*. Oxford: Berg

Valdez-Tullet, J. (2019). *Design and connectivity: the case of Atlantic rock art*. Oxford: British Archaeological Reports

Vandkilde, H. (2017). *The metal hoard from Pile in Scania, Sweden*. Aarhus: Aarhus University Press

Versaci, M. (2019). *El sol, símbolo de continuidad permanencia: un estudio multidisciplinar sobre la figura en el arte esquemático de la Provincia de Cádiz*. Oxford: Archaeopress

Vourc'h, M. (2011). Experimentation and technological analyses in the study of the rock carvings at the site of Hjemmeluft, Alta, Finmark, Norway. In E. Anati (ed.), *Arte e communicazione nelle società pre-letterarte*. Milan: Jaca Book Spa, pp. 476–85

Vyner, B. (2007). Rock art in Cleveland and north-east Yorkshire. In A. Mazel, G. Nash & C. Waddington (eds.), *Art as metaphor: the prehistoric rock art of Britain*. Oxford: Archaeopress, pp. 91–110

Wehlin, J. (2013). *Österjöns skeppssättingar. Monument och mötsplatser under y yngre bronsålder*. Gothenburg: Gothenburg University Institute for Historical Studies

West, M. (2007). *Indo-European poetry and myth*. Oxford: Oxford University Press

Westlake, S. (2005). Routeways and waterways: the Neolithic / Bronze Age rock carvings on the Dingle peninsula, south-west Ireland from a landscape perspective. *Archaeological Journal* **162**, 1–30

Wickler, S. (2019). Early boats in Scandinavia: new evidence from Early Iron Age bog finds in Arctic Norway. *Journal of Maritime Archaeology* **14**, 183–204

Wilcox, A. (1984). *The rock art of Africa*. London: Routledge

Winter, L. (2008). From diffusion to interaction: connections between the Nordic area and Valcamonica during the first millennium. In H. Whittaker (ed.), *The Aegean Bronze Age in relation to the wider European context*. Oxford: British Archaeological Reports, pp. 35–55

Wrigglesworth, M. (2006). Explorations in social memory: rock art, landscape and the reuse of place. In R. Barndon et al. (eds.), *Samfunn, symboler og identitet*. Bergen: Universitet i Bergen, pp. 147–62

Wrigglesworth, M. (2015). Between land and water: the ship in Bronze Age west Norway. In H. Stebergløken et al. (eds.), *Ritual landscapes and borders within rock art research*. Oxford Archaeopress, pp. 111–8

Acknowledgements

This Element is a selective account of a large body of material that is usually considered on a local scale. It reviews the main styles of rock art found in Europe between the Mesolithic period and the Iron Age and considers their wider significance for prehistoric archaeology. It is aimed at a wide audience of prehistorians rather than specialists on ancient imagery and considers how studies of this kind can contribute to broader discussions in European archaeology.

I must thank Manuel Fernàndez Götz and Bettina Arnold for inviting me to write it and Aaron Watson for the figure drawings. I am grateful to Lara Bacelar Alves, Stephen Cogbill, Ramon Fàbregas Valcarce, Courtney Nimura, Aaron Watson and Cecilia Dal Zovo for providing photographs and for allowing me to use them. I am also grateful to Lara Bacelar Alves, Cecilia Dal Zovo, Ramon Fàbregas Valcarce and Peter Skoglund for commenting on a draft of the text.

The Element is dedicated to Courtney Nimura and Peter Skoglund, with whom I have worked so happily in the field.

Cambridge Elements ≡

The Archaeology of Europe

Manuel Fernández-Götz
University of Edinburgh
Manuel Fernández-Götz is Reader in European Archaeology and Head of the Archaeology Department at the University of Edinburgh. In 2016 he was awarded the prestigious Philip Leverhulme Prize. His main research interests are Iron Age and Roman archaeology, social identities and conflict archaeology. He has directed fieldwork projects in Spain, Germany, the United Kingdom and Croatia.

Bettina Arnold
University of Wisconsin–Milwaukee
Bettina Arnold is a Full Professor of Anthropology at the University of Wisconsin-Milwaukee and Adjunct Curator of European Archaeology at the Milwaukee Public Museum. Her research interests include the archaeology of alcohol, the archaeology of gender, mortuary archaeology, Iron Age Europe and the history of archaeology.

About the Series
Elements in the Archaeology of Europe is a collaborative publishing venture between Cambridge University Press and the European Association of Archaeologists. Composed of concise, authoritative, and peer-reviewed studies by leading scholars, each volume in this series will provide timely, accurate, and accessible information about the latest research into the archaeology of Europe from the Paleolithic era onwards, as well as on heritage preservation.

E
A   European Association
A   *of* Archaeologists
A

Cambridge Elements ☰

The Archaeology of Europe

Elements in the Series

A Comparative Study of Rock Art in Later Prehistoric Europe
Richard Bradley

A full series listing is available at: www.cambridge.org/EAE

Printed in the United States
By Bookmasters